CAT'S CRADLE

CAT'S CRADLE

CHIEKO N. OKAZAKI

Bookcraft
Salt Lake City, Utah

Library of Congress Catalog Card Number: 93-72857
ISBN 0-88494-904-4

First Printing, 1993

Printed in the United States of America

To Ken and Bob

Contents

PART ONE

Love and Service

1

"Count Me Therefore a Partner"

*D*o you remember making a cat's cradle when you were a child, and how magical it was to turn a long, straight piece of string into a complex and connected pattern? Do you remember how each part supported the other parts and was connected to them? Each part was essential. You could not make one part more important than another without destroying the whole pattern.

Not all parts of the cat's cradle have the same job, but all parts are essential. The pattern takes many turnings, some expected and predictable, others surprising. I like to think of the Spirit of the Savior as filling the spaces between the string, making it possible for the pattern to appear. And I think something special happens everywhere the strings cross and touch each other. Those crossings are relationships; and I want to address myself particularly today to the partnership relationship of men and women.

This address was delivered at a husband/wife evening, Willow Creek Stake, Sandy, Utah, on 9 September 1992.

The title "Count Me Therefore a Partner" comes from a lovely incident in the New Testament, one of the shorter letters of Paul, which he writes to a wealthy member named Philemon, asking him to receive back a runaway slave and to be kind to him. Both the wealthy member and the slave are converts to the Church. Note how warmly Paul urges Philemon to consider this slave as a brother in the gospel:

> Not now as a servant, but above a servant, a brother beloved, specially to me, but how much more unto thee, both in the flesh, and in the Lord[.]
> If thou count me therefore a partner, receive him as myself.
> If he hath wronged thee, or oweth thee ought, put that on mine account. (Philemon 1:16–18.)

When I think about partnership, I think about my own marriage, so I'll want first to tell you about Ed and the cat's cradle of love and shared responsibility we had in our partnership. Then I'll talk about how these principles also work in Church assignments.

My Partner Ed

It is a source of sorrow to me that you cannot know my husband, Ed. He was stricken with a cardiac arrest just hours after the Relief Society sesquicentennial broadcast in March 1992, and he died six days later without regaining consciousness. His death interrupted forty-two years of a tremendous partnership in marriage and Christian living. I know no one is perfect—and Ed was not perfect either—but it's hard for me to think of anyone who is a better example of service, love, and generosity.

I met Ed at the University of Hawaii, where we were both students. He had fought in Italy and France during World War II as part of the 442nd Regiment, which was made up exclusively of Japanese-Americans. To those who doubted their loyalty to the United States they proved it by becoming the most decorated unit in the United States Army. They also had the highest casualty rates of any unit. Ed was awarded the Silver Star for bravery and spent a year recuperating from the wounds he suffered. So you could say that Ed was a hero and had the medals to prove it, but he wasn't aggressive or reckless or attracted to violence. He was motivated by a desire to serve, by loyalty, and by love. Those were dominant characteristics in his personality.

Ed was a Congregationalist and I was a Latter-day Saint when we met. From the beginning, I recognized his immense generosity of spirit, his deep kindliness, and his devotion to Christ. Many people counseled me against marrying out of the Church, and I gave the matter much prayer and consideration. I knew that Ed was an honorable man who loved the truth. I felt he had the heart to accept more truth when he learned it. I was very encouraged when he stopped smoking and drinking while we were going together. I felt almost sure that he would join the Church, but I still asked myself searching questions: If Ed never joins the Church, can we still have a good marriage? Do we have enough respect, enough love, enough similarity of goals to be happy together? I felt that the answer was yes, so we were married; and ten months later Ed joined the Church.

We were married in 1949. This was a time when the United States was booming. Post-war prosperity made it possible for millions of Americans to improve their standard of living, own their own homes, get good educations, and raise their families comfortably. It was also a time when women left the jobs they had taken to help win the war and went home to split-level ranch houses in the suburbs and drove station wagons full of children to ballet lessons and Little League games. It was a time of togetherness and material prosperity that worked very well for some marriages but which made specialists out of most couples: the husband specialized in earning the living and the wife specialized in rearing the children.

If it had not been for the gospel, Ed and I might have tried to fit into the same pattern there in Hawaii as our brothers and sisters were doing. But because we were the only members of the Church in our families, we had to cling tightly to each other and work out our own rules as we went along, especially when we moved to Salt Lake City in 1951. Ed was working on his Master's of Social Work at the University of Utah and I was the first exchange teacher from Hawaii at Uintah Elementary School. Because of medical problems, conception was difficult, and we were very grateful when our son Ken was born after four years of marriage. Robert, seventeen months later, was a medical surprise to the doctors and a wonderful surprise for us. I had stopped teaching when Ken was born; but my principal at Uintah found herself shorthanded and begged me to return—just for a year.

At that point, Ken was four and was in nursery school. Robert was three. Ed and I talked it over seriously and decided we could manage it. Ed was especially encouraging. He said, "Chick,"—that was his nickname for me—"we may not be able to have other children, and you know that you love teaching. It's just a matter of time until you'll go back to the classroom again, and you may not have such a wonderful opportunity later." So we investigated and found a loving woman to tend Robert, and I went back to Uintah School.

We knew this decision meant that we couldn't follow the specialization model that many of our neighbors were using, and that the change would mean quite a lot of differences to our family. But because we both wanted to make those changes and create a situation that would work for our family, it was not a difficult change. Even when I had not been working, Ed had participated fully in parenting. The boys were his number one job, just as they were for me, and now that I was working they were the number one job for both of us. The number two job was everything else—our work, our Church assignments, and our housekeeping chores. That one year worked so well that it became reasonable to ask, "Why not continue?" So we did.

Both of us did housework. Both of us cared for our boys and played with them. Both of us planned our time so that we could be with them as much as possible. Both of us arranged our other commitments and our Church jobs to include them as much as possible. If one of them was ill, we took turns missing work to be nurse. And, almost unbelievably, neither child ever had a long-term or complicated illness. We took turns going to the boys' schools for programs, teacher conferences, or sports events. I do not recall those years as stressful. We just did our best and didn't worry about the rest.

We always supported each other in our Church callings, but our time of working most closely together came in 1968. Ed and I were called to preside over the Japan Okinawa Mission, and Ken and Bob were teenagers. As you know, women in traditional Japanese society are expected to be very retiring and inconspicuous in public life; and some of the members interpreted their understanding of the priesthood in a way that reinforced this traditional understanding. At church, too, they expected women to be withdrawn and submissive while the men made the decisions. Because I was president of all of the auxiliaries in the mission, Ed had me attend the mission presidency meetings with his two Japanese counselors, both to explain about the work of the auxiliaries and to take the minutes. He patiently taught the principle of shared partnership and, after everyone became used to it, all was well.

It was a great delight to Ed and me when the sisters in the mission finally stopped hanging back to make a shy bow in deferential silence but instead came forward, shook hands with a smile, and greeted Ed with all of the news, questions, and information they had to give him. I saw the priesthood leaders and sisters working together with new trust and confidence in each other. The little branches grew strong enough to support the mission's leap in baptisms from eighteen the first month we were there to more than two hundred a month three years later. Elder McConkie, who was our mission supervisor, gave Ed and me a compliment we have always cherished when he told us, "You two are a *team!*" We felt like a team, and we loved being a team.

About five years later, when we were back in Denver, Ed said to me, "You know, Chick, you've been teaching for twenty years and you've still got fifteen years before you retire. Have you ever thought about becoming a principal?"

I said, "Ed, how could I go back to school? I'm fifty years old!"

He just smiled and said, "Then you can't start any sooner, can you?"

I thought about what he had said and the idea was very appealing. I had worked on enough committees and task forces to know that I liked organizing and was good at helping people work together. The boys were in college, and I was ready for a new challenge. So I decided to go for it. With Ed's support, I received my M.A. from the University of Northern Colorado in 1977, and my Administration Certificate from Colorado State University in 1978. It wasn't easy. Doing the course work meant night school, and the University of Northern Colorado was a two-hour drive away. Ed patiently cooked his own supper and spent those evenings alone without complaining. He always asked me how I was doing, took on even more chores around the house, and when I got my degree, he was smiling even more than I was!

I share these stories, even though they make me miss Ed very much, because I want you to understand two principles that worked so well to create a partnership in our marriage. I believe that these same principles also operate when men and women work together in the Church. First, a partnership focuses on the best way to do the task, not on who gets to give the orders. Second, a partnership always builds strengths in both partners, even though each partner has different strengths.

Goal-Centered Partnership

Think of a family in which the father and the mother never consult the children about which chores they'd like to do or how they'd like to do them. Is that a system that works very well for the children? What I'm trying to say is that partnerships need to be goal-centered, not authority-centered. Often we think of order and organization and structure as a ladder. When I had snow piled so high on my roof during the winter that I worried, our friend, Paul Seppi, a roofing expert, came to check it for me. He brought his ladder because he wanted to climb up.

A ladder is a very useful tool because it leads in both directions. It got Paul up on the roof, and then it brought him down.

But in our minds we often see ladders as leading in only one direction. If we're at the top of the ladder, we think only about the people who are lower than us on the ladder and how we need to keep a flow of instruction going down that will keep them organized. If we're on the lower rungs of the ladder, sometimes we feel nearly washed away by that flood of instructions and it often seems very difficult to interrupt that flow long enough to say, "But wait! I have a concern," or "I want to ask a question!" And sometimes the person one rung above you will listen to your question but never pass it on. Or if the question goes up the ladder from person to person, sometimes you can't recognize the answer when you get it back. And sometimes an answer never comes back. Does any of this sound familiar?

The priesthood organization builds clarity and simplicity. This is its great strength. But other arrangements have other strengths. When you're thinking about ways to build partnerships in your families and in your Church assignments, think less of ladder arrangements and more of my cat's cradle. A network is more complicated, but I think it's also more flexible and more supportive.

In the meetings between the Relief Society General Presidency and our advisors, I get a cat's cradle feeling. Take the literacy effort, for example. Our meetings are a structure that we five people created to focus on the goal of how literacy can benefit some members of the Church. Our meeting time with our advisors is ours alone, every single month, regularly and reliably. We sisters bring the agenda, and there's time in the meeting for all of us to talk and all of us to listen. After we discuss some matters, our advisors tell us to go make our own decision. Other matters require their involvement in the decision-making process. And still other matters require them to get more information from the larger priesthood system to bring back to us. But we are all focused on literacy and how it can meet the needs of some members of the Church.

Let me also give you a professional example. In one school

where I was principal, we handled a lot of difficult issues for the district. We were a year-round school, and we also had four different tracks to meet the different needs of children on different levels. Sometimes our teachers felt overwhelmed by the complexity and fatigued by so many demands. They would say things like: "We just can't do it. It's too complicated. It creates problems in reporting to the district. We have to work out new schedules every term."

I would always listen to everything they had to say, and then I would say something like this: "I understand that there are problems with the schedule and problems with reporting to the district when our program doesn't fit any of the categories they already have. It would probably be simpler for the district if we reported their way, too. But let me ask you a different question. What is best for the children?"

The results were nearly always the same. When the teachers began thinking about the children—about the people they were supposed to serve—and not about the chain of command or the system imposed on them from the outside, they nearly always found good ways to solve the problems. And solving the problems was worth the effort it took because they had reminded themselves that their goal was to serve the children.

Let me suggest, then, that one way to build partnership between the priesthood and the Relief Society and between men and women working together in any organization in the Church is to concentrate on the task. Instead of trying to match handbooks or align lesson manuals, ask, "What is best for the children in our Primary?" or "What is best for the youth of our ward?" Of course it's important to ask, "What is the program?" but it is more important to ask, "What would meet the needs of the older people in our ward?" or "What is best for the single mothers?"

Who's important in our ward? It's the people we serve—the children or youth or adults whom we teach, those to whom we provide leadership, even the person sitting next to us in sacrament meeting who needs a warm smile and a cheerful word. Elder Marion D. Hanks, our advisor until the summer of 1992, taught us this principle with a wonderful story.

A few months earlier, during the ceremonies of unveiling the new Aaronic Priesthood statue, Elder Hanks told us about his visit to a certain stake conference. As usual, he asked to speak briefly to the children between the ages of three and six, who were having a separate meeting while their parents were in stake conference. He came in, met the Primary president, and sat down, escorted by the stake president and counselors. The Primary president, in introducing him, said: "Children, we have some very important people here with us today. Who can count how many important people are here?" One little girl on the front row enthusiastically waved her hand, and the Primary president said, "Can you count the important people who are here?" The little girl jumped up and turned her back on the Primary president, the stake presidency, and Elder Hanks. Beginning at the child in the seat next to hers, she began carefully counting all of the children, "One, two, three, four . . ." The Primary president was embarrassed, but Elder Hanks was simply delighted.

People-centered partnership is a cat's cradle approach. It doesn't create ladders and then look for people who are at the top. It focuses on the goal of serving the people who are closest to us and asks what is best for them.

Individual Strengths

The second point I want to make about partnership is that a partnership always tries to build strengths in both partners and that each partner usually has different strengths. I am not a weak person, and Ed was not afraid of my strengths. I supported Ed completely in his profession as a social work administrator, and in his Church work, as a Scoutmaster (three times!), counselor in a bishopric, high councilor, mission president, and Regional Representative. He did the same for me in my profession as an educator and in my Church callings. That meant we coordinated schedules, analyzed personnel, accommodated each other's busy seasons, thought through problems together, used each other for sounding boards, asked hard questions and insisted on answers, and prayed with and for each other. Ed expected me to be strong, he praised me for being strong, and he encouraged me to be even stronger.

I remember once in Denver he came home from a hard day at the office—he was regional associate commissioner of the Commission on Aging—and wearily explained that he'd spent the entire day working with widows who were so shattered by their husbands' deaths that they could barely function. He commented, "I wonder how those husbands felt, knowing they were leaving wives who were completely unprepared to take care of the children and make decisions." Then he smiled at me and said, "If anything should ever happen to me, Chieko, I know that you understand our finances, that you know how to get help, that you could take care of the boys, and that you'd carry on."

I've thought of that statement so often since he's been gone. I think Ed's faith in me is one reason why he encouraged me to reach for the top in my profession and to be the best kind of educator I knew how. What if he had said: "I'll take care of it. Don't worry about it. Let me do it. You don't need to know or do or understand this." He would have been giving me two messages. One would have been, "I love you and I want to take care of you." But the other would have been, "I *have* to take care of you because you can't take care of yourself."

It is partly because Ed expected me to be strong, to not be overwhelmed by sorrow, and to carry on that I have felt motivated to dig deep enough to continue with my responsibilities. My sons and I sorrowed greatly and still do, but we can bear it. After his death, I was scheduled to visit every stake in Hawaii, plus BYU—Hawaii, conducting women's meetings and workshops, in an eleven-day tour. People wondered if I would do it, if I *could* do it. When they asked me, I said, "The Lord's work does not stop." So I went forward with it. I was uplifted by the love of the sisters in Hawaii, and I felt Ed with me in special ways. I don't think I would have had those same experiences if I had been weeping alone in my house in Salt Lake City.

Or what would he have communicated if, in Japan, he had said, "My counselors don't think much of women and I'm afraid they'll be rude to you, so I don't want you to come to these meetings." Instead he communicated to me: "We're partners. We're in this together. We'll take the criticism together, and we'll work to change things together."

When I needed to travel to visit the auxiliaries, he never said: "Oh, I don't want you traveling alone. Wait until district conference." I never wanted to be away from home longer than necessary, so I would take the late train back from a conference, travel all night, and be home in time to cook breakfast before the boys went to school. Ed knew that was important to me; and instead of saying, "Oh, stay overnight at a hotel and take the train back the next day," he would quietly arrange his own schedule to accommodate mine.

Now, when men and women work together in church, how can they build strength in each other? We've already talked about the first way, and that's to be a goal-centered team, where the focus is on the task, not on who is in charge. Think again about the cat's cradle. A ladder always assumes that the person on the higher rung is the stronger person, but that's not necessarily so. In a cat's cradle, you can't even ask that question because the string is the same strength all the way around. When we're working out the pattern of a cat's cradle, we pay attention to the moving part, the part that needs to change to form a new pattern—but when it's done, all parts of the pattern are equally beautiful and equally important.

But I think that the most important way to build strength in partners is to realize that our real job is relationships; people, not programs; ministering to others rather than just administration. Building strong partners means that you trust your partners, even if they don't do everything perfectly. I think it means respecting their decisions and their intentions, even if their behavior isn't perfect yet. It means kindness, nurturing, and appreciation.

It will be easier for us to be strong partners and build strong partnerships if we keep focused on our real job—and that's the same as the Savior's—to "love one another" (1 John 4:11). I remember reading an article, I think in the *Ensign*, about a college student in a modern dance class. Her teacher assigned all of the class members to do a particular exercise one day. They had to begin at one point in the studio, go to a second point, and finish at a third point. They could move in any way they wished between points—leaping, rolling, spinning. Whenever they encountered another class member on the way, they had to stop and have some kind of interaction: they could dance together for a few minutes, pantomime a fight or a flirtation—anything that involved an action and a response. Everyone in the class was assigned three different points, so their paths crisscrossed in very complicated ways.

This student was very determined to show the teacher how beautifully she could make leaps or pirouettes to reach her three points, but she became very frustrated because she kept encountering other members of the class and was obliged to interact with them. She felt terribly exasperated when the time for the exercise elapsed and she still hadn't reached her third point. And then she learned that the teacher didn't care if they never reached even the second point. The teacher was interested in the creativity and responsiveness of the dancers' interactions as they encountered each other. Those things the student thought were interruptions were the only important activities going on.

I feel that the Lord may have similar interests. He must shake his head in disbelief as he watches us zooming past each other, very intent on our meetings and our schedules and our lists, when what he wants us to do is pay attention to each other and the human needs of each heart. Mother Teresa tells her sisters, "The work is only a way to put our love for Christ into action."[1] I think that's important for us to remember when we feel that only the work is important. Remember the love. Love builds strengths.

Our real work is relationships. When we understand this, every contact creates and enriches and reinforces a relationship. It's a ripple effect; but the ripples, instead of dying out, get stronger. Ed understood this principle perfectly. Ed's cardiologist, Dr. Robert Fowles, spent hours with us and Ed at the hospital during those terrible six days when Ed was dying. He said: "This is just as difficult for me as it is for you. Ed is not just a patient. He is my dear friend." I knew that what he said was true as he shared our grief and did not try to hide his own. After Ed's death, he wrote such a warm and cherishing letter to me, saying: "Anything I can do for you would be a privilege. Please call me." His relationship with Ed extended beyond Ed to me and the boys in a cat's cradle of caring and sharing. It is a richer relationship because it is not a ladder relationship.

Paul Seppi is a fine workman. I think of him every time I notice that our roof is *not* leaking during a rainstorm. But we don't have just a business relationship with Paul. It didn't end when we handed over a check in exchange for a mended roof. Ed talked with Paul while he was working and found out that Paul was planning to go pick up his son, who was finishing a mission in Tokyo. Ed knew how difficult it was to find lodging at a reasonable price, so he wrote to friends in Tokyo and asked if Paul could stay with them for two or three nights. We are connected with Paul's son as well as Paul's roof.

These networks of connections cannot happen with ladders, because as soon as someone changes places on a ladder the relationships change, too. It is a great joy to me to be back in Salt Lake City again, because I encounter the children of our missionaries and the children of my former students. The connections extend even into the second generation now. But in a ladder relationship, I would be only the teacher. When a second-grader moved into the third grade, poof! our relationship would be over. One day as I was talking to a hostess in the Relief Society building, she said, "I feel that I know you because my husband and his son have talked about you." I had taught her stepson in 1951, long before she married the father, and it made a connection between the two of us. I feel the strength of those relationships.

President Barbara B. Smith in 1976 said: "All that the Brethren have taught me says that we have a companion relationship—not inferior or subordinate, but companion, side-by-side. The priesthood presides, but each of us contributes a vital part to make the whole complete. This isn't my plan. It's the Lord's plan."[2]

That's certainly the feeling I had with Ed and it's certainly the feeling I have in working with our priesthood leaders in my Relief Society calling. I like what President Kimball has said about men and women in marriage. I think it also applies to men and women working together in the Church. Let me paraphrase his statement about marriage to apply to our broader Church circumstances: "When we speak of [Relief Society] as a partnership, let us speak of [it] as a *full* partnership. We do not want our LDS women to be *silent* partners or *limited* partners in that eternal assignment! Please be a *contributing* and *full* partner."[3]

Now, how do we make partnership work? Let me tell you a story related by Thomas W. Ladanye, a therapist and an institute director, about the power of communication in marriage. He said:

In one of our Institute faculty meetings at the University of Michigan some years ago, I was asked to conduct a husband-and-wife communication session. Prior to our meeting, I asked two colleagues to try a little experiment with their wives and children and report their experience at the meeting. Both agreed; one even said he would record the dialogue between him and his wife. The assignment I gave them was quite simple—they thought! Each was to sit down with his wife in a private situation where they wouldn't be interrupted and ask a simple question, "What can I do to improve our relationship?"

One couple had been married for thirty years, the other for eighteen; and both of the marriages were happy ones. Each husband agreed cheerfully to carry out the assignment and seemed confident that it would be relatively easy.

At the faculty meeting a week later, I called on the younger man first. He was a jovial, outgoing guy, fun to be with and always kidding around. As he stood up to respond, however, he was unusually subdued. Quietly he said, "You know, when Tom gave me this assignment, I thought it would be easy. Millie and I have a great marriage and a great relationship. I was even taping it; I was so sure of her response. But when I asked, 'What can I do to improve our relationship?' I was shocked at her answer.

"She began by saying, 'Hal, you're a wonderful person and a

good father and husband, but—' and then she proceeded to bombard me with a lot of pent-up feelings she had been holding within her for years. I never knew she felt that way, and she had never told me because she didn't want to hurt my feelings or the time never seemed right."

They had talked well into the night; and perhaps for the first time in their entire eighteen years of marriage, they had discussed some very meaningful issues in depth. He concluded by turning to me and saying, "Thank you, Tom, for helping open my eyes."

The second man, also a close personal friend, reported a similar experience. "I assumed after thirty years of marriage that I knew my wife," he said simply. "But I was wrong." He had taken her to a nice restaurant for dinner and asked the question during a leisurely moment.

"Helen stopped eating," he said, "grabbed my hand, and burst into tears." He was flabbergasted and embarrassed but even more concerned and shocked about her response. She also told him she loved him very much but—and then followed some deep and emotional feelings about the "incompleteness" of their relationship. Their conversation lasted through dinner, all the way home, and late into the night. He was surprised and enlightened by his wife's response.

Both of these fine men and their wives indicated that they learned a great deal from this experience and vowed they would ask that simple question more often—and listen hard to the response. The second couple, based on this experience, later asked each of their children this very same question; and in one case, the father and one son healed a long-painful relationship by getting to the root of the problem.[4]

This therapist was obviously recommending that husbands ask this question of their wives, but wives can ask their husbands how they can be better wives and start the discussion that way. I don't see any reason why the same question will not work with colleagues, among presidencies, and between visiting teachers and sisters being visited. Just ask, "What can I do to improve our relationship?" The sincere desire to serve—to minister to another's needs—opens doors in a powerful way.

Conclusion

Partnership is a topic close to my heart. It taps some very tender feelings as I think about my own partner. If we sometimes feel stuck on a ladder, let's think about ways to change it into something more like a cat's cradle, something that will let us focus on the goal. Let's be innovative and creative as we explore ways of building partnership, not only in our marriages and with our children but also with friends and colleagues as we work together as men and women in building the kingdom. Remember that not one of us needs to pull the load alone. We can help each other, and the Savior will help us when we do.

And finally, remember that true partnership strengthens both partners. It focuses on ministering to people, not just administering the program. Whatever our assignment or task may be, our real job is the Savior's work—to love each other and show it in ways that make others stronger.

Ed was a wonderful example of how to do this, and he continues to inspire me. I think that he may continue to help me even now. About five months after Ed's death, I was lying in bed early in the morning just before I needed to get up to go to an early meeting. I wasn't asleep. I was just relaxed. And I heard Ed call me, "Chick! Chick!"

It was exactly what he used to do when he got out of the shower and I was still in bed. He wanted to be sure that I wouldn't oversleep and miss getting up on time. Oh, I jumped right up and called, "Ed!" There was no answer, of course, but I felt so good!

Ever since he died, I'd been wondering where he is, whether he knows what's happening with me and the boys, and I so desperately wanted just a little contact with him again. And so this was how he chose to come. I have to smile. It's so characteristic of Ed. Just a loving little service. If he had come when I was desperate with sorrow and loneliness, when I felt bewildered and sure that I just couldn't cope, it's possible that I might have thought, "He came because he knew I couldn't manage without him." He knew I *could* manage, and so he let me struggle through those hard times—and they're by no means over. But this little service, a loving support to help me with my calling, is exactly the service that Ed would have chosen to perform in life.

My dear brothers and sisters, there is a world that needs our work; and we will work better in partnership. Our families will work better, and the Church will work better. With the Apostle Paul, let's say, "Count me therefore a partner," and work together "for the perfecting of the saints, for the work of the ministry, for the edifying of the body of Christ: till we all come in the unity of the faith, and of the knowledge of the son of God . . ." (Ephesians 4:12–13).

Notes

1. José Luis González-Balado and Janet N. Playfoot, My *Life for the Poor: Mother Teresa of Calcutta* (San Francisco: Harper & Row, Publishers, 1985), p. 7.

2. Barbara B. Smith, "A Conversation with Sister Barbara B. Smith, Relief Society General President," *Ensign*, March 1976, p. 11.

3. Spencer W. Kimball, "Privileges and Responsibilities of Sisters," *Ensign*, November 1978, p. 106, italics in original.

4. Thomas W. Ladanye, *Speaking from the Heart* (Midway, Utah: Quest 2001, 1991), pp. 22–23.

2

Love from the Beginning

*W*hen my husband and I took our last vacation together in Hawaii before his death, we went to the big island of Hawaii, where I grew up. The tiny village where I was actually born, Hoea, is no longer there. Cane fields cover it. But in Mahukona, the slightly larger village where I spent my childhood, I found the clustering of homes where about fourteen Japanese families lived and the plank sidewalk that connected our neighborhood with the Hawaiian neighborhood. I never felt isolated there, perhaps because there were so many children in the locale and also because all of the parents had the same standard. None of us ever tried to tell *our* mothers that "Noriko gets to stay up till ten," because we knew better.

Down on the beach, I found the children's swimming pool. It was a place where my father had arranged rocks to let the water into a fairly flat-bottomed area. The water was deep

The original version of this address was given at women's conferences in Honolulu Stake, 21 April 1992, and at Hilo Stake, 29 April 1992, with other portions taken from a ten-minute general address given in Japan and Korea in October 1992.

enough that we children could actually learn to swim, but we could still find our footing and the rocks broke the force of the incoming waves. We swam every day, just as hard as we could, in perfect safety while we were little, then later ventured out beyond the rocks into the ocean, where we gained the confidence and skill to tumble about in the surf like dolphins and swim with joy in the deep water.

Some aspects of growing up came to me early. When I was fourteen, I went to Honomakau, where I worked as a maid for board and room so I could go to school. Honomakau was the beginner's pool for me. The faith and confidence of my parents in my ability and the good habits and skills they had taught me were the great rocks that broke the force of the incoming waves of fear, even when I was alone.

Honolulu was deep water to me. When I graduated from high school and the next step was college, I took it with eagerness and anticipation but also with great trepidation. I left home at the end of the summer of 1944, during World War II. The interisland transport system was hardly luxurious then. I remember that I had to take a cattle boat from Hawaii to Oahu. My parents and my little brothers came down to the dock to see me off. As my mother hugged me good-bye, she whispered, "*Gambare!*" Do you know this Japanese word? It means both *Carry on!* and *Don't give up!* Later, Ed and I used it as the informal slogan for our missionaries; and by then, our California elders had the perfect translation for it: *Hang in there!* I actually like that translation better, because it acknowledges that times are going to be rough.

So I came to Honolulu and the University of Hawaii with my mother's "*Gambare!*" in my ears and in my heart. I had never been to such a big city before, but I truly loved it. I loved attending our meetings in the Mission Branch in McCully District with the other students. I met Ed two years later when the war had ended and when he had spent a year recuperating in the hospital. By the time we graduated, we were engaged.

That was a time of beginnings for me, and love was in each of those beginnings: my father's love for us children, my love for learning, my sense of the Savior's love and my love for him as I discovered the gospel, and the new love that was growing between Ed and me as life companions. In 2 John 1:1–6, a beautiful scripture, John talks about "love from the beginning." He is writing to a woman whom he identifies only as the "elect lady," and tells her, "I beseech thee, lady, not as though I wrote a new commandment unto thee, but that which we had from the beginning, that we love one another." This whole passage is a lovely one:

> The elder unto the elect lady and her children, whom I love in the truth; and not I only, but also all they that have known the truth;
> For the truth's sake, which dwelleth in us, and shall be with us for ever.
> Grace be with you, mercy, and peace, from God the Father, and from the Lord Jesus Christ, the Son of the Father, in truth and love.
> I rejoiced greatly that I found of thy children walking in truth, as we have received a commandment from the Father.
> And now I beseech thee, lady, not as though I wrote a new commandment unto thee, but that which we had from the beginning, that we love one another.
> And this is love, that we walk after his commandments. This is the commandment, That, as ye have heard from the beginning, ye should walk in it.

I want to talk about this commandment from the beginning, the commandment to love that sprang from the very heart of Jesus and which is the very heart of the gospel. Perhaps this principle of the gospel is especially dear to me because I grew up in Hawaii where the Saints of the many Polynesian islands have come together in the spirit of aloha. They seem to understand almost instinctively the great treasure and joy of love. I think of this ability to love as a great gift for the rest of the Church. The internationalization of the Church means a sharing of gifts. Saints around the world will learn the lessons that the Saints of Hawaii already seem to know—lessons about valuing differences, cherishing diversity, not judging others, and loving stead-fastly.

So today, let's talk about three miracles of love: first, the ability of love to see the individual; second, the transforming power of love; and third, the patience of love.

Love Sees the Individual

The first point I want to make is that love sees individuals, not groups. That's why love doesn't get discouraged when it is confronted with literally thousands of homeless people on the streets of Calcutta, with thousands of abandoned babies, with old people and sick people dying in corners with no one to take care of them. Love is a Mother Teresa who sees one individual, one at a time. Love does not despair that there is no hospital. Love gives a cup of cold water and gives the even more precious gift of letting a dying man close his eyes on a loving face as his last sight in mortality.

As reports have come in to the Relief Society about the service projects with which the sisters have celebrated the sesqui-centennial, we have been delighted at the creativity, the service both to groups and to individuals, and the way sisters have given what they had to give.

One of the most inspirational and meaningful lessons from the scriptures, in my view, is the story of Jesus healing the blind man. I have learned four important lessons from this one story from the perspective of how love sees the individual:

> And as Jesus passed by, he saw a man which was blind from his birth.
> And his disciples asked him, saying, Master, who did sin, this man, or his parents, that he was born blind?
> Jesus answered, Neither hath this man sinned, nor his parents: but that the works of God should be made manifest in him.
> I must work the works of him that sent me, while it is day: the night cometh, when no man can work.

As long as I am in the world, I am the light of the world.

When he had thus spoken, he spat on the ground, and made clay of the spittle, and he anointed the eyes of the blind man with the clay,

And said unto him, Go, wash in the pool of Siloam, (which is by interpretation, Sent.) He went his way therefore, and washed, and came seeing. (John 9:1–7.)

First, Jesus was probably surrounded by dozens of people from the time he got up that morning. We know that at least twelve people were around him. But the narrative singles out one man—one man with a problem—whom Jesus encountered almost by accident. Jesus hadn't gotten up that morning and said, "Oh, boy, Tuesday! Time for a service project." He wasn't looking particularly for this blind man. Nor had the blind man made an appointment to see Jesus. No one had brought him to Jesus or put him in Jesus' path. Many of our opportunities to serve come in just the same way, almost as a chance encounter with a single individual who needs help of some kind.

Second, the disciples were interested in the man as a case of speculative theology. They wanted to know about the cause of the ailment. Was he blind because he had sinned or because his parents had sinned? They asked Jesus to explain this man's situation. They wanted to use him for an example, a visual aid. The record doesn't say whether they knew him or even greeted him—just that they considered him to be an interesting case. And Jesus answered their question, giving them a mini-sermon, not only about sins but also about himself as the light of the world. However, that's not the important point for me. What strikes me is that Jesus saw something they didn't. He saw the need of the individual. He looked beyond the man as an example, as a "case," and he saw that the man needed to have his sight restored. The disciples looked at a man and saw blindness. Jesus looked deep into those blind eyes and saw—not a visual aid, not an example—but just a man.

Sometimes I think we see programs. We count the Lord's sheep instead of feeding them. We check to see how many chairs are filled, not who is filling them and—even more important—who is missing. We see groups instead of individuals. We see cases instead of the person. Let's follow the example Jesus sets us—of always looking deeply into the eyes of the person who encounters us on the road. If we can see who is there— even if the eyes are blind—then we truly have vision.

Third, Jesus performed the service immediately. He had miraculous powers which we ordinarily lack, but I think that the model is still good for us. He didn't have a lot of fancy equipment. He didn't transport the man to an exotic medical facility. He didn't organize a cornea transplant team. He didn't make it into a media event. He used the resources he had, that minute, and acted on the spot. He spat in the dirt and mixed up some mud. He put mud on the man's eyes, and it was enough.

Sometimes we think that we can't serve because we're "too" something—too young, too old, too rich, too poor, too unhappy, too busy. In essence, we say to the blind man, "Wait right here. I'll be back just as soon as I read up on the right kind of mud and get a sterile mixing bowl and a chemically inert spoon." We don't need to do that. Jesus' example liberates us from those demands to be more. Who we *are* is enough. If love sees the other person as an individual, it also makes us feel our own individual worth, our individual power, our individual ability to make a difference.

Fourth, Jesus' service gave the blind man a way in which to exercise faith. Jesus didn't just dump the service on him and walk away. Instead, he told the blind man to go wash in the pool of Siloam. Jesus was taking a risk, wasn't he? What if the blind man had sat there saying, "Wait a minute. What's going on here? You put *mud* on my eyes? That's disgusting. You must be some kind of a nut!" And, if the blind man had reacted that way, he might have stayed blind. Instead, he got up, probably with mud caking and falling off on his face and clothes, and groped his way to the pool. The combination of Jesus' service and the recipient's faith—which Jesus gave him a chance to exercise—made the miracle. So the man "washed, and came seeing." We don't even know that man's name, but millions of people know his unique story. Jesus' love transformed him from one blind man among thousands of people in Jesus' world into a unique individual.

The Transforming Power of Love

And that's my second point: the blind man stopped being an interesting theological case study and became a miracle because Jesus loved him.

Now, let's think of another case: the story of Zacchaeus. Let me tell you this story.

> And Jesus entered and passed through Jericho.
>
> And, behold, there was a man named Zacchaeus, which was the chief among the publicans, and he was rich.
>
> And he sought to see Jesus who he was; and could not for the press, because he was little of stature.
>
> And he ran before, and climbed up into a sycomore tree to see him: for he was to pass that way.
>
> And when Jesus came to the place, he looked up, and saw him, and said unto him, Zacchaeus, make haste, and come down; for to day I must abide at thy house.
>
> And he made haste, and came down, and received him joyfully.
>
> And when they saw it, they all murmured, saying, That he was gone to be guest with a man that is a sinner.
>
> And Zacchaeus stood, and said unto the Lord; Behold, Lord, the half of my goods I give to the poor; and if I have taken any thing from any man by false accusation, I restore him fourfold.
>
> And Jesus said unto him, This day is salvation come to this house, forsomuch as he also is a son of Abraham.
>
> For the Son of man is come to seek and to save that which was lost. (Luke 19:1–10.)

Isn't this a fascinating and mysterious story? We see Zacchaeus climbing the tree, Jesus looking into the tree and calling him down, and then all of them going into his house. I assume that the door closed behind them, and outside stood the grumblers who couldn't imagine why Jesus wanted to be with a sinner. And then suddenly, Zacchaeus reappears giving away half of his property and restoring fourfold what he had cheated. What happened behind that closed door? What changed Zacchaeus? The story doesn't tell us, but let's imagine what might have happened. There's a wonderful commentary on this particular experience by Barbara Howard that I'd like to share with you:

> Picture [Zacchaeus], if you will, peering through the leaves, eyes aching with a hunger for a response to the faith stirring in him. Then—there Jesus is! Standing at the foot of the tree, Jesus looks right up into Zacchaeus's face. And Zacchaeus, looking down into the face of this holy person, sees himself reflected in Jesus' eyes. What that despised tax collector sees is not what the crowd sees—"the one who is a sinner." He sees a man beloved, of value, capable of responsible action, freed, whole.
>
> In the eyes of Jesus, Zacchaeus saw the person God created him to be. That is the power of unconditional love—the power to reflect back to us the best of ourselves. Think about your own life for a moment. Remember the times when you have been loved without requirements, but loved just because you are. Remember . . . how you felt about yourself when you accepted that love. . . .
>
> I have a friend who was for many years distanced from her family and from her faith community. . . .
>
> She tells the story about coming home for the celebration of her grandmother's retirement. There was a great deal of judgment from her parents, her brothers and sisters, uncle and aunts. She felt cast out even as she tried to draw into the family circle. Then, she said, she stepped onto the porch of her grandmother's house and her grandmother walked out the front door.
>
> "In that moment," she said, "I was home. I looked in my grandmother's eyes and saw the woman I was capable of being. Grandmother put her arms around me and in her embrace I knew that I was forgiven and I could be the person I truly wanted to be."
>
> . . . Jesus did not say to the tax collector, "Zacchaeus, if you will do the following list of requirements, I will invite you to come down and will go to your house today." Unlike those who stood by and grumbled, Jesus offered Zacchaeus a new image by accepting Zacchaeus unconditionally.

A wonderful ancient story from the Near East illustrates this principle:

Once a holy man was invited to a dinner party by a wealthy patron of the town. When evening came, the holy man appeared dressed in his usual tattered robe and shabby turban. His host, startled by the holy man's appearance, turned him away at the door. The holy man thereupon went to another wealthy friend and borrowed much more respectable attire, returned to the party, and was welcomed with lavish cordiality. Sometime later, other guests were puzzled to observe the holy man sitting alone in the corner, occasionally mumbling something into his sleeve and then dropping into it sweetmeats and other delicacies. The host drew close and heard the holy man mumble, "And this is for you," into the sleeve. The host inquired about the strange behavior, to which the holy man replied, "It is only right that I should do this: after all, it is the robe and turban who were really invited here."

The encounter between Zacchaeus and Jesus is not measured by externals. Reflected in Jesus, Zacchaeus found his inestimable value. "I must stay at your house today" was Jesus' way to embracing all of Zacchaeus' life—his past, his present moment, and his future.[1]

Sometimes we make it very hard for people to come to church. We want them to be righteous before we agree to accept them as our brothers and sisters. But this is not how Jesus behaved and this is not what he said. When people asked him why he associated with tax collectors and sinners, he said, "They that are whole need not a physician; but they that are sick. I came not to call the righteous, but sinners to repentance," or as a modern translation puts it: "I have not come to call the respectable people to repent, but the outcasts" (*Good News for Modern Man: The New Testament in Today's English Version* (Nashville, Tenn.: Broadman Press, 1966), Luke 5:31–32). We need to give our love to anyone who needs it, not keep Zacchaeus up in the tree waiting to become perfect before we call him down.

Aren't there moments of transforming love in your own life? Perhaps it was your mother or father who loved you so, a teacher, a wife or a husband, a missionary, or a child's innocent love. You know how you feel about that person. But if we have ever been on the other end, if someone has ever come to us and said, "You changed my life," you know that it was not your own words, your own values, your own intellect, your own ability to understand the world, or your own love that made such a difference in that person's life. Rather, it was the love of the Savior, filling your heart, brimming over into that other person's life, and creating the change.

The Patience of Love

The Apostle Paul tells us that love "suffereth long, and is kind; . . . seeketh not her own, is not easily provoked, . . . beareth all things, . . . endureth all things" (1 Corinthians 13:4–5, 7).

I want to tell you a story about a patient woman with a loving heart—Elizabeth Alina Keopuhiwa Fong. I knew some of the businesses that the Fong family of Honolulu was engaged in and so I was delighted to learn more about Alina in the *Proceedings of the Mormon Pacific Historical Association*. According to her granddaughter, Elizabeth Lim, Alina was born in 1894 in Pauoa, Honolulu, to a Hawaiian mother and a Chinese father, the oldest of their four children. She had a few years of schooling but began working at age twelve in the Dole Pineapple Cannery. "Because she was such an honest and efficient worker, it wasn't long before someone . . . asked her to come and work for the Wo Hop Steam Laundry, the first Chinese steam laundry in Hawaii, located near the present Kawaihao Church in the Kakaako District."

Her first impression of the boss, Fong Hing, was that he was "rather stern and serious looking." She was fourteen, and he was thirty-four, which seemed very old to her. She tried to be very inconspicuous because she was afraid of him, but he quickly "noticed this quiet, hard-working young lady who spent her coffee-breaks and lunch hour either reading, crocheting, or doing something worthwhile. 'This was an unusual girl—so young in years and yet so mature in mannerisms,' he thought." She was about fifteen when Fong Hing sent his cousin to her

father's home to propose marriage. Alina's father left the decision completely up to her, and she decided that "she would
marry this hard-working, serious, though somewhat elderly
man, because she felt he would be a kind and thoughtful husband, a good father for her children, and in her own words—
'not run around.'" They were married on New Year's Eve in
1910; and after the wedding luau, Alina immediately returned
to the laundry and finished the jobs that had to be delivered to
the ships scheduled to leave in the early morning.

She had certainly recognized her husband's business acu-
men. He branched out, opening a jewelry store, a bondsman
business, a restaurant, a general merchandise store, and a mat-
tress company. Fifteen children were born to them in twenty
years. During World War II, rather than moving to the mainland for safety, Alina and Hing purchased a large home on Victoria Street as a sign of their faith in the Allied victory. Now
two large condominiums stand on the site of her home, Victoria
Plaza.

Alina had been a member of the Church all her life; and her
"greatest moment of joy" came when her husband joined the
Church at age seventy-one. She had spent "thirty long years of
hoping and praying" that he would join her in her religious faith,
even though it seemed impossible "that he'd ever take time to
think of a God, let alone accept Him." But in 1946 he asked her
to "teach him about her God." He said that she had reared all of
the children "untiringly and without any complaints and that he
didn't think anyone could do such a job without some help.
Then he said; 'It must be your God that helped you. I want to
follow your footsteps and learn about Him.'"[2]

I celebrate Alina's patience. Sometimes our love is impatient. We want quick answers and hasty solutions. Sometimes
we feel such urgency that we would violate the free agency of
others. This is not a mistake that our Heavenly Father and Jesus
make. Their love is deep and powerful but it is also a patient
love. For every Paul struck down on the road to Damascus, for
every Alma the Younger who is rebuked by an angel, there are
hundreds who are allowed to go on choosing and choosing and

choosing, until a series of choices gradually leads them to make the right choice and the hunger of their spirits for the Holy Spirit makes the gospel sweet to them.

Another story I love about the necessity for patience is *The Little Prince*, written by the French writer Antoine de Saint-Exupéry. It tells of a little prince who lived on a very small planet, where his special friend was a rose. This was the only rose he had ever seen, and he thought she was the most beautiful thing in the universe; so when he came to earth and saw whole gardens full of roses, he was thunderstruck and upset. He decided that he had been wrong in his admiration of his rose, and that she was not so special after all. But then a fox taught him an important lesson about the patience of love.

When the little prince asked the fox to play with him, the fox said he could not, because he had not yet been tamed. The little prince asked: "What does that mean—'tame'?"

The fox explained that, right now, they didn't know each other or need each other. There was nothing unique about the fox to the boy or about the boy to the fox. But taming would create a bond, a need for each other, a recognition of their uniqueness. "Other steps send me hurrying back underneath the ground," said the fox. "Yours will call me, like music, out of my burrow. And then look: you see the grain-fields down yonder? I do not eat bread. . . . The wheat fields have nothing to say to me. . . . But you have hair that is the color of gold. Think how wonderful that will be when you have tamed me! The grain, which is also golden, will bring me back the thought of you. And I shall love to listen to the wind in the wheat."

The little prince hesitated. Did he have time to tame the fox? He had so much to do, so much to see, so much to understand. Then the fox said something profound and true: "One only understands the things that one tames."

So the little prince agreed to tame the fox and asked him to explain the process:

> "You must be very patient," replied the fox. "First you will sit down at a little distance from me—like that—in the grass. I shall

look at you out of the corner of my eye, and . . . you will sit a little closer to me, every day. . . ."

The next day the little prince came back.

"It would have been better to come back at the same hour," said the fox. "If, for example, you come at four o'clock in the afternoon, then at three o'clock, I shall begin to be happy. I shall feel happier and happier as the hours advance. At four o'clock, I . . . shall show you how happy I am! But if you come at just any time, I shall never know at what hour my heart is to be ready to greet you."

So the little prince tamed the fox, but he was perplexed and sad when it came time to leave and the fox wept for sorrow. He wondered if taming the fox had done any good at all. The fox assured him that it had, and then told him: "Go and look again at the roses. You will understand now that yours is unique in all the world."

So the little prince once again went to look at the garden full of roses. And now he understood something. He knew that his rose was unique. His rose was more important than all of the other roses because he understood this rose.

Then the fox told him three secrets. First, the fox said, "It is only with the heart that one can see rightly; what is essential is invisible to the eye." Second, "It is the time you have wasted for your rose that makes your rose so important." And third, "You become responsible, forever, for what you have tamed. You are responsible for your rose."[3]

These are secrets that cannot be learned quickly. We learn them only when we are patient and steadfast in our loving. When we learn that "it is only with the heart that one can see rightly," we develop spiritual eyes to look upon the inward person. When we do this, we will discover a wonderful secret: Every person is, as it were, the Savior in disguise. In every person, we will see the divine son or daughter of God for whom Jesus Christ suffered and died. And with such a view, how can we help loving each other?

The fox's second secret was this: "It is the time you have

wasted for your rose that makes your rose so important." Many times we feel the pressure of our administrative burdens so intensely that we feel we do not have the time or strength to also minister. Remember the parable of the Good Shepherd? He took the ninety and nine to a safe place, then left them to go into the wilderness, by night, calling for the lost sheep. What the parable does not tell us is how the ninety and nine felt. Perhaps they felt lonely. Perhaps they wished the shepherd were there to sing to them as the moon rose. But I think each sheep must have thought, "If I were lost, if I had gone astray, the shepherd would come look for me, too, just as he is looking now for the one who is lost." That kind of message is more assuring even than presence, because it is a promise for the future. Remember, when you attend lovingly and perceptively to the needs of just one you also minister to the ninety and nine.

The third lesson of the fox is this: "You become responsible, forever, for what you have tamed." When you have established a special relationship by spending time with someone and learning to know that person's heart, you become responsible for him or her. She is no longer just one more sister to visit. He is no longer one more member of the elders quorum. He or she is someone special, and has claims on you forever, and vice versa. You cannot suddenly say, "Oh, someone else has been assigned to be your visiting teacher. I will not visit you any more." Your heart will tell you that you must be consistent in cherishing and nurturing that relationship, otherwise the person will know that you were just doing a duty and that there is no real love in your heart for him or her.

In all things, it is our Savior who sets the example of patience in love. First, he clearly sees our heart. Second, he has all the time in the world for us. He is always available to us through prayer, and his Spirit is our constant companion if we will have it so. And third, he is responsible for us forever. He promises, "I will never leave thee nor forsake thee . . . I am with you alway, even unto the end of the world" (Hebrews 13:5; Matthew 28:20).

Conclusion

My dear sisters and brothers, may our love never fail. May we learn truly to look upon each individual with the eyes of love so that we can see a person, a son or daughter of God, a sister or brother to us. May we become instruments of the transforming love of our Heavenly Father, so that through us others may see themselves as Heavenly Father sees them and know that they have the ability to become great. And finally, may we be patient. May we be patient with ourselves, patient with each other, and patient as the great pattern of the Lord works itself out in and through our lives.

Notes

1. Barbara Howard, "Faithful Discipleship," *Saints Herald* 138, no. 11 (November 1991), p. 16.

2. Elizabeth Lim, "A Mormon Family in Hawaii," in *Proceedings of the Second Annual Conference, Mormon History in the Pacific, May 8–9, 1981, Brigham Young University—Hawaii Campus* (Laie, Hawaii: Mormon Pacific Historical Society, 1981), pp. 109–12.

3. Antoine de Saint–Exupéry, *The Little Prince*, translated by Katherine Woods (New York: Harcourt, Brace & World, 1943), pp. 63–71.

3

Feeling the Rhythm

*S*ervice is a wonderful principle of the gospel—maybe even my favorite. I'd like to share three ideas about service. First, service is a process. It's not a product, and it's not a project, even though we use both images to think about service. Second, service brings joy as an inevitable and environmentally enhancing by-product. And third, service, even if you're doing it with twenty thousand other people, is still an individual activity.

Service as a Process

When Gary Trost, the center on Brigham Young University's basketball team, made the highest scores of his career in March 1992, he didn't even know he'd done it. When the reporters told him,

---

This address was delivered at Y Day, Brigham Young University, Provo, Utah, 6 April 1992.

his eyebrows shot up in surprise, and he appeared at a loss for words. He almost looked embarrassed. Finally he said, "I was just trying to work hard."

Then he gave it some more thought and added, "Usually when I start out well it gets me going. I started feeling the rhythm. . . . I just wanted to play solid."

. . . One thing that helped open it up for Trost inside was the perimeter shooting of guard Nate Call. . . . And naturally, Trost gave Call credit for that help.[1]

It's clear how Gary's experience applies to service. He achieved his record-breaking results not by focusing on the product but by focusing on the process. He wanted to work hard. He felt the rhythm of what he was doing. And he played with a team, not as a solitary star.

What do I mean by the rhythm of service? For some people, service isn't a rhythm like the running, pivoting, passing, and shooting that Gary Trost was talking about. It's complicated and difficult. They think about all of the conditions that have to be in place before we can serve. They say: You have to be called. You have to be assigned. The service has to be on this checklist of eighty-seven approved projects. You have to have the right credentials. You have to put in so many hours. You have to be sure that it has such-and-such an outcome. You have to organize at least ten other people to do this same service.

Well, I have a much humbler view of service. It's not complicated at all. You see a need—you meet that need, just as quickly as you can, doing the very best you can right at that moment with the resources that you have. That's the rhythm: see and act. Perceive and do.

I want to teach you an important Japanese word, *kigatsuku* (pronounced key-got-soo-koo). I'll let you in on a little secret. *Kigatsuku* has the same number of syllables as *Hallelujah*. So if you know Handel's "Hallelujah Chorus," you can just plug in *kigatsuku* instead.

Kigatsuku means an inner spirit to act without being told what to do, a willingness to serve, a self-motivated impulse toward goodness. I was a teacher and a principal for thirty-three years altogether. In that length of time, one learns a lot about service and how to serve others. The five third-graders at Wasatch Elementary who are having trouble learning the times tables don't need a legislative subcommittee called to study the educational outputs of seven hundred representative third-graders in Arizona, New Jersey, and Nebraska. They need someone to sit down with them, just the five of them, and sing, "Four times one is four, four times two is eight, four times three is twelve," maybe thirty times, until it sinks in right to the bottom of those little gray cells. You don't need a Ph.D. You don't need to set time aside for a two-week seminar. You don't need to plan a seventy-question survey for evaluation purposes. You just need to know the times tables and have ten minutes to spend with those five third-graders. Rhythm. Think of the rhythm. See a need, meet a need.

Don't feel that you are not old enough, not educated enough, or not rich enough to serve. Don't worry too much about product or the outcome. Feel the rhythm of seeing needs, of meeting needs. We can trust that rhythm. It's the Savior's own rhythm. Can you hear how he tells us in this scripture to relax, to fall into step with him?

> Thou shalt have a gift if thou wilt desire of me in faith, with an honest heart, believing in the power of Jesus Christ, or in my power which speaketh unto thee;
>
> For, behold, it is I that speak; behold, I am the light which shineth in darkness, and by my power I give these words unto thee.
>
> And now, verily, verily, I say unto thee, put your trust in that Spirit which leadeth to . . . do justly, to walk humbly, to judge righteously; and this is my spirit. (D&C 11:10–12.)

Feel that desire to serve in your own heart and respond. Know that the desire comes from the power of Jesus Christ. Trust that spirit. Believe that if you see a need and stretch out your hand to meet it—even if your hand is empty—believe that the Savior will give you the gift you need to complete that service, even in the act of reaching out. So that's point number one: feel the rhythm of service. Think of it as a process, not as a product or a project.

The Joy of Service

Second, I want to talk about the joy of service, a joy that is woven into the fabric of my life in the Church. April 6 is one of the most special days of each year for me. Sure, we all know that the Church was organized that day, but that's not what I mean. It's the anniversary of my baptism in Kohala, Hawaii, in 1942. It was a sunny day, a simple ceremony. There were just four of us. There were the two missionaries, Elder Merrill Jenkins and his companion, and Sister Sakai, a woman in her thirties or forties. We drove to Niulii, Kohala, eight to ten miles from Honomakau, where I was going to school. In the gymnasium where the Saints met was a redwood box, smaller than a regular baptismal font, that the missionaries filled with cold water. I had brought my own white dress to wear. There were no local members there, no speeches of welcome, no instructions in our duties as members, no choir, no visiting dignitaries, no refreshments— just an opening song, an opening prayer, and a few remarks from the missionaries. We were baptized and confirmed. Then we drove back to Honomakau.

It was a very hard day for me; but at the same time it was a day of great peace. I had been investigating the Church since I was eleven and had been praying for the past several months about joining the Church. This was just four months after the Japanese Imperial Air Force had bombed Pearl Harbor, you remember. The United States was at war with Japan. I was living away from my parents and working as a maid so that I could go to high school. Otherwise, my education would have ended. My parents were Buddhist but had not opposed my involvement with the Mormons because I had always gone to Buddhist services and performed the Buddhist rituals in our home—but for any child to depart from the religion of her parents is hard for the parents. I had made this decision on my own, and now I was going home to tell my parents. That was the hard part.

But the peace came from the clarity. In praying about what to do, it had become clearer and clearer to me that this was the Church of Jesus Christ. I had a testimony of Jesus Christ, and I could not turn my back on it. I heard no voice. I saw no vision. There was no miracle that compelled my belief or that forced me to act. I was given knowledge and then I was left free to choose. In looking back on it now, I am as grateful that Heavenly Father respected my agency as I am grateful for the clarity of knowing. I felt trusted. I felt that I was acknowledged for who I was.

When I went into the waters of baptism, I had a simple view of my life. I saw myself as living in Hawaii for the rest of my life, being a good and faithful member of the Church, and, if my dreams came true, of teaching school. I never imagined that I would come to the mainland. I never imagined the opportunities to serve that would come to me. And I would not have believed them if I had seen, somehow, an image of myself in the future. Sister Sakai lived that life. She remained a faithful member of the Church there in Kohala. Her husband was not a member, but that did not stop her from gently, quietly, consistently serving. That could have been my life, too. And that would have been a wonderful life. But the Lord had other plans in mind. The gospel literally changed my life. My heart was changed. I accepted Jesus Christ and Heavenly Father. I now knew about a God that I believed in and could talk to and felt a kinship with. I felt loved and trusted. I became a new person. I saw myself in a new way. I accepted new goals and ideals as part of being a Christian and a Mormon. I was hungry for knowledge, thirsty for service, and the gospel satisfied that hunger, that thirst.

I'm sure we have all read many times the injunction of Alma to earlier converts at the Waters of Mormon, as recorded in Mosiah 18:8–10. Let me slightly reword these instructions so that they apply to us, who are already baptized members of the Church:

> We are desirous to stay within the fold of God, and to be called his people. We are willing to bear one another's burdens, that they may be light;

Yea, and are willing to mourn with those that mourn; yea, and comfort those that stand in need of comfort, and to stand as witnesses of God at all times and in all things, and in all places that we may be in, even until death, that we may be redeemed of God, and be numbered with those of the first resurrection, that we may have eternal life—

Now, I say unto you, *is* this the desire of our hearts? For we have been baptized in the name of the Lord, as a witness before him that we have entered into a covenant with him, that we will serve him and keep his commandments, that he may pour out his Spirit more abundantly upon us.

Do you remember the response of the people? "They clapped their hands for joy, and exclaimed: This is the desire of our hearts."

Well, I think extraordinary things happen when service and spirituality become the desire of our hearts. Neither one of these things is flashy or glamorous; but those of us who have tasted both know that nothing is sweeter or stronger than the joy that results.

Let me tell you about my husband. Ed is the most *kigatsuku* person I know. It was the rhythm of his life. Being attuned to others was a reflex with him. People have told me lots of stories about Ed since his death, stories that I never knew but which haven't surprised me. One of our missionaries said a friend of his was attending a meeting of volunteers to help in a particular candidate's campaign and told him—the missionary—the next day at work: "I was sitting by the nicest man. He was older, Japanese, and we just started talking before the meeting began. Nothing special, but he was just so pleasant to be with." Our missionary knew that Ed was interested in this particular candidate and asked his friend to describe this man. It *was* Ed. Now, Ed's purpose in being at the meeting was to find out how to help the candidate's campaign. But the fact that he was sitting next to someone a few minutes before the meeting started was an opportunity he couldn't pass up because Ed has always been intensely interested in other people. So they chatted for a few minutes. Was that a service? Well, obviously it was. Ed's pleasant, courteous interest was so great a service to that other, young volunteer that he spontaneously mentioned it the next day in conversation to a colleague—who just happened to be one of our missionaries.

One more example. The week before Ed died, I accepted an invitation to speak on service in a ward Relief Society sesquicentennial celebration. The Relief Society president was married to one of our missionaries. Ed accompanied me. A few days later, after Ed had died, this sister called me and said, "I thought you'd like to know. I was sitting where I could see Ed's face during your talk. He was paying such close attention and enjoying it so much. Then afterwards, while the sisters were crowded around you, I lost sight of him. When I looked again, there he was, quietly folding up the tables and chairs and putting them away." I think the sisters got two lessons in service that day— one from my talk and one from Ed's example, first in supporting me so totally by his attention and next in quietly seeing a need and fulfilling it.

I have to say something else about Ed. He was the happiest man I know. Part of it is that he had a very sunny disposition, was always cheerful, and looked on the bright side. But part of it is connected with his almost instinctive service, the rhythm of seeing needs and meeting needs, the reflexes for righteousness that he developed.

If I could give you a gift, it would be to give you this same joy in service that Ed felt. To him, it wasn't a chore or a duty or a responsibility. It was a joy. I'm sure you've heard dozens of lessons and heard hundreds of talks about the importance of service and the joy it brings. But what if the joy isn't there? What then? Well, at that point, we often make a terrible mistake. We feel wretchedly guilty and redouble our efforts, make longer lists, have worse experiences and reproach ourselves more. We take on more projects. We work more anxiously toward some product. We keep checking on how we feel. We focus on ourselves or on having the longest service list. And the joy gets further away.

Is your service a joy or a job? Sometimes we over-program

ourselves. We take on too much. We take on things that are too elaborate. We become so weary in doing good that we can no longer do it well.

I feel that service is a duty and a responsibility, but it is also voluntary, not compulsory. If your service is starting to feel like a job, then you need to change things to get the joy back. I think that often the problem is that we are no longer choosing. We are not seeing needs. Someone else is. And we are not responding to the need of an individual whose need we see. We're responding to a third person who has noticed the need and who is assigning us to take care of it. We are product oriented on the task instead of process oriented on the rhythm of seeing a need, meeting a need. We are not person oriented on the individual.

Let me remind you of the principle of agency. Often we say yes to our bishop or to a list being passed around in Relief Society or to a speech that makes us feel guilty. What we should be saying yes to is a need that we ourselves see in a real person—friend, spouse, child, or stranger.

So if the joy feels like a job, see if you need to reevaluate your circumstances. You know what your resources are and the demands on them. There come times in every life when there's just nothing left to give. King Benjamin gave us a model to follow here: "I would that ye say in your hearts that: I give not because I have not, but if I had I would give" (Mosiah 4:24). Accept that you are in a season of depletion, and do not add guilt to your burdens as you wait for renewal.

I'm not talking about fear. We sometimes want to say no to a calling or an assignment out of fear—because we're afraid that we can't do it right. When we have to struggle with fear, let's pray for more faith. "I can do all things through Christ which strengtheneth me" (Philippians 4:13). A second reason why we sometimes want to say no is out of selfishness. When we have to struggle with selfishness, let's pray for more charity, the pure love of Christ. But if we come to a season in life when King Benjamin's counsel applies to us, let's pray to really know our limits and our priorities.

We're counseled not to run faster than we have strength

(see Mosiah 4:27). Let's look at our own circumstances, appraise our own strength, get in touch with our own desires. Let's not let someone else tell us who we are, what we can do, and how we should feel about it. When we do, there's no joy in our job and we can't feel *kigatsuku* about our service. Let's keep our own agency. Let's choose freely and wisely.

Let's also remember that all kinds of service are acceptable to the Lord. We may think that service is getting out there and collecting funds for a children's orthopedic unit or a homeless shelter. Sometimes it is. But sometimes it's writing out the check for the volunteer who comes canvassing, and saying sincerely, "Thank you so much for giving your time to do this. I hope that someday I can do the same thing." If we're in a life season when a serious responsibility is not for us, let's look for little services to perform.

I remember reading about the Mormon high school students in Lathrop High in Fairbanks, Alaska, who made a difference just by providing "smiles, friendly attitudes, and leadership qualities." Another teen commented: "One thing I noticed when I first met these kids is that they all smile. It's like they know something you don't. They walk through the halls with a grin on their faces, most of them. It makes you kind of wonder, why are they so happy all the time?" She found out why when she joined the Church: "I guess the gospel kind of does that to you."[2]

Nephi was able to serve and not question or resent his father. How did he become that way? Why did Laman and Lemuel become the way they were? They were raised in the same family, the same city. They were exposed to the same teachings. I think it has something to do with free agency. The process is missing—the Book of Mormon doesn't document it— but we can work backward and figure out part of it.

What process did Nephi choose? Nephi chose a close relationship with his father. He chose to listen to him, believe him, consult with him, and desire to be like him. As a result, he made other choices. He chose to trust the Lord and feel loved by the Lord. These choices constructed a reality—a reality in which his father was a prophet and in which the Lord led and guided his family. Laman and Lemuel chose a different reality and ended up with a different set of consequences. They didn't trust the Lord. They didn't feel loved by the Lord. They constructed a reality that led them on a distorted path. Both Nephi and Laman said yes to some things, no to other things. Know that you have the same eternal right and responsibility to choose. And choose wisely, so that the things of greatest value have the highest priority. So that's my second point: in addition to feeling the rhythm of service—seeing a need, meeting a need—let's be *kigatsuku,* choosing freely and responsibly, so that our service stays a joy, not a job.

Service Is Individual

The third point I want to make is that service, even if you're in a project that involves twenty thousand other people, is still an individual activity. Sometimes it's hard, when we're involved in a group project, to see who we're serving. Sometimes our service becomes impersonal. Of course, it's important that we write out those checks for fast offerings and slip them in the contribution envelope. It's important that we drop our spare change into those canisters at the grocery store for multiple sclerosis research. It's important that we contribute our old magazines to an elementary school project. But it's most important that we find ways to serve personally—to look into other eyes, to touch other hands, to see the needs we are meeting.

I was very impressed by this insight when I read a statement by Susa Young Gates, who was concerned about the Relief Society's attempt during the early 1920s to professionalize its compassionate service. "To give money," she stressed, "is the cheapest kind of service—to give love and personal services is the most difficult of all impersonal tasks."[3]

Professionalism and professional services are crucial; but some things are best done by amateurs. Let me put it to you: Do you want your husband or your wife to be a professional in love-making with experience gained through long, general training, or do you want an amateur who specializes just in you? God seems to feel that the best parents are amateurs—just two ordinary people and an ordinary baby, learning about each other and teaching each other simultaneously. Jesus didn't seek his Apostles among the nation's most highly trained theological professionals. He seemed to feel that twelve ordinary men were good enough.

Kigatsuku isn't a professional quality and it can't be taught as part of professional training. Instead it comes from an educated heart. It's triggered by seeing a human need. It sees human beings as supremely important—not in groups but just one at a time. Ed was this way. When Ed was working as a psychiatric social worker at the VA Hospital in Salt Lake City just after he got his MSW from the University of Utah, he would go on the rounds with the doctors. As he walked down the hallway, he greeted all the workers. "Hello, Joe," he'd say to the man washing the windows. "Hello, Annie," to the woman who was scrubbing and mopping. "Hello, Elsie," to the file clerk at the counter. He knew everybody who was doing menial tasks.

The doctor asked, "How do you know these people? How come you know them by name?"

Ed said, "I make it a point to know them. These people help keep the hospital running, and they need to know that they're important. I want them to know that I'm here to help them if there's anything I can do."

When Ed was made state director of aging services, his department had a big party for him, open to anyone who wanted to come. That place was crowded with all the people who did the menial and mundane tasks. They came and shook his hands and hugged him and I heard them say things like, "Who will ever talk to us again? Who will ever call us by our names?" I think Ed and I have been blessed to understand people who are downtrodden and to see people who need our help. We want to give them our understanding and our empathy.

Some service projects are noisy, active, demanding. But if there are quiet moments when you're working next to someone, remember that you have a special opportunity to give the gift of love. Ed would have laughed if anyone had told him that there was something sacrificial and redemptive about his enthusiastic, happy interest in other people. But there was. The power of love anywhere, anytime, is transforming and redemptive. When you're working next to another, talk to each other. Ask to hear each other's stories. Find out what is important to each other and share the same things about yourself.

And please, please, don't think that you have nothing to share or that nobody wants your interest. All of us—in the community formed by our shared commitments to the gospel—need the individual differences that come from our diversity. I had a wonderful experience reading a recent address by Elouise Bell, an English professor at BYU and a convert to the Church. She shared some profound thoughts about how we can all enrich our gospel unity by our individual diversity: "We can speak of the Mormon *faith*, meaning the Mormon religion or belief system. We think of that as a relatively fixed, formed set of concepts. But when we speak of an individual's *faith*, what we are talking about is a totally unique thing, as individual as fingerprints or memories."

Elouise describes how her own faith had grown as a result of working with the diaries and journals of Patty Bartlett Sessions, a Mormon pioneer midwife and healer. Elouise gives a one-woman show of Patty's experiences as a spunky, energetic, old woman talking to the other women clustered around the bed-side of a woman in the early stages of labor. Elouise comments: "By feeling the spirit of this remarkable woman, I have been strengthened and uplifted and renewed. Patty's faith, which was at any given time the composite of her unique life experiences, has fed my faith."

Another exemplar of faith for Elouise is Corrie ten Boom, who is also one of my favorite Christian women. She was Dutch and, during World War II, with her father and sister turned their home into a refuge for Jews. They were betrayed and sent to a concentration camp. Her father and sister died. Elouise says Corrie's "book, and the movie, *The Hiding Place*, tells the story of that particular and amazing faith. At the end of the film, the real Corrie, now old and immensely powerful, as full of zeal and faith as anyone I have ever seen, looks straight at the camera and fixes it, and us, with her piercing eyes as she gives us her testimony. Corrie ten Boom has strengthened and uplifted and contributed to my faith. My faith is not her faith, however, and my faith is not Patty Sessions' faith, any more than I am a banana because I have eaten crates of bananas in my life."

Then Elouise points out:

> My faith has been blessed by many who are neither Mormons nor Christians. It would take at least another speech to tell what I owe to Jewish women and men of strong faith. The spirit and faith of Native Americans have bolstered my faith, shored up my faith, with pillars I had not found anywhere else. Certain rays of light from eastern religious traditions have illuminated and enriched my faith. . . .
>
> Today, The Church of Jesus Christ of Latter-day Saints is daily adding to its numbers men and women from every corner of the globe, some with little in the way of previous faith, it is true, but many with mature and seasoned faiths of a composition little known to nineteenth-century Mormons, or even to most contemporary Saints. From Africa, from Asia, from South America, and from Eastern Europe, the Church is gaining members with experiences, backgrounds, insights, and wisdom that have not been available to us as a church body before. What a wonderful day this is! What pillars of faith these people will be able to share with us! And certainly, we would be most unwise, not to say unrighteous, were we to say to the spiritual insights these new saints bring: "We have no need of thee."[4]

I say with Elouise Bell, "We have need of each other." I've shared stories about myself and about my husband because I hope they will help. We all have stories to share. We all are unique. You may think that you grew up in absolutely the most typical family in Orem, Utah, or led the most unexciting life ever experienced in Pocatello, Idaho. You long to know the stories of really exotic people from Zimbabwe or Paris or Seoul.

What Elouise is saying is important: your faith is unique. Your experiences are like no one else's. Every day is a day the Lord has made—a day to offer the service of appreciating another as a unique difference. During lunch breaks or while you're standing in line at the grocery store, make a connection with the person next to you. And listen to those who share the same stories with you. Respect and rejoice in the differences as in the commonalties. The whole Church will be stronger for the understanding you will gain. Service is individual. Your service is unique because you're a unique individual. And whoever you are near today is a unique neighbor to you.

Conclusion

In conclusion, then, we've talked about three ideas. First, service is a process. It's not a product, and it's not a project. Second, it's a joy, not a job; and sometimes you need to make a different set of choices from those around you to be sure that it's still a joy. And third, service, even if you're doing it with twenty thousand other people, is an individual activity. Whatever the assigned service task, the real service occurs in your interaction with the people nearest you.

It is a joy to remember Ed in the context of service. Ed's world was filled with loving people because that's the kind of person he was. He always saw needs and joyously met them. As a result, he was surrounded by helpful, loving people who were concerned about him. It's a matter of rhythm—of righteous reflexes, of choosing the sweetness of service rather than the quick fix of selfishness and gratification. Listen to your own spirit. Feel those tender feelings and act on them, not expecting a reward.

And as we do so, I supplicate our Heavenly Father to bestow on all of us the love which is his gift to "all who are true followers of his Son, Jesus Christ; that [we] may become the sons [and daughters] of God; that when he shall appear we shall be like him, for we shall see him as he is; that we may have this hope; that we may be purified even as he is pure" (Moroni 7:48).

Notes

1. Richard Evans, "Cougars' Trost Stuns Even Himself with Career Game," *Deseret News*, 8 March 1992, D1–D2.

2. Larry Hiller, "Mormon Corner," *New Era*, March 1992, pp. 28–29.

3. Susa Young Gates, as quoted in Janath R. Cannon and Jill Mulvay Derr, "Resolving Differences/Achieving Unity: Lessons from the History of Relief Society," in *As Women of Faith: Talks Selected from the BYU Women's Conferences*, edited by Mary E. Stovall and Carol Cornwall Madsen (Salt Lake City: Deseret Book Company, 1989), pp. 129–30.

4. Elouise Bell, "Yet All Experience Is an Arch," *Sunstone*, 15, no. 5 (November 1991), p. 19.

4

Circles That Include

*W*henever I speak to a group of sisters, I see in the eyes of some a question: "What do we have in common? You don't even know me." Sometimes these unspoken questions come from sisters who are struggling with many little children and who were doing well to find a pair of pantyhose that hadn't been snagged on a tricycle. What does such a woman see when she looks at me? She sees a woman many years away from that stage of child-rearing. It's been a long time since I said to myself, "I'd better not wear these dangling earrings, or as soon as I pick up the baby I'm going to lose the earring and probably part of my ear, too!" Do I have something in common with that sister?

I see the same question in the eyes of women who are struggling with other aspects of their lives—with poverty, with illness, with singleness, with feelings that they may be different from the

Portions of this address were given at a singles fireside in the Mount Vernon Washington Region, 9 February 1992, under the title, "Circles That Include"; at Monument Park Stake women's conference, Salt Lake City, Utah, 20 June 1992, under the title, "Circles of Love"; and at Pilgrimage, a women's retreat, in Salt Lake City, 2 May 1992.

sisters who *really* make up the Relief Society. They look at me and think, "If that's what I'm supposed to look like, act like, or achieve like, I don't think we have very much in common."

Well, my dear sisters, we have the most important thing of all in common—a shared testimony of the Savior. And perhaps there are aspects of our experiences that we share as well. What will you remember about the Relief Society sesquicentennial? For me, it will always be associated with the death of my husband. He was stricken with a fatal heart attack within hours after the sesquicentennial broadcast from the tabernacle. Are you a widow? We have that aspect of our lives in common?

Many sisters have experienced great adversity in trying to get an education and raise their children. My parents were humble laborers on a Hawaiian plantation, and I put myself through high school by working as a maid for my room and board, and also worked my way through college.

Perhaps you are a convert? My family is Buddhist. I was baptized a Latter-day Saint at the age of fifteen without their permission, though they later consented. Some of you know what it is to have part-member families. I am still the only member of the Church in my family, and my husband, Ed, was a Congregationalist when I married him. Perhaps there are days when you feel overwhelmed by the demands of juggling family and work responsibilities? I worked most of my married life, first as an elementary schoolteacher and then as a principal, so I know the kind of balancing act that is required.

Perhaps ill health is a serious burden for you. I am a triple cancer survivor and know what is involved in coming close to the edge of death. Being Japanese by ancestry has not always been an advantage in the United States of America, and perhaps you also know the pain of racial prejudice or another form of discrimination.

Of course there are many ways in which we are alike, but I want you to know these things about me, because I think each point of connection with someone else is a spiritual strength to us. Even though we always have the gospel in common, it sometimes feels as though that cannot be enough if there is no one else who understands how you feel. In high school many years ago I memorized a little poem by Edward Markham called "Heretic":

> He drew a circle that shut me out;
> Heretic, rebel, a thing to flout.
> But love and I had a wit to win;
> We drew a circle that took him in.

Circles of Inclusion

Do we know how to draw circles of inclusion, not circles of exclusion? Have any of you ever felt shut out by a circle that seemed to include others who had no more particular right to be there than you? It hurts, doesn't it? It feels unfair, doesn't it? And in contrast, you know how it feels to be in the circle.

We all have a human need for belonging, for closeness. Groups fill that purpose. The Church fills that purpose. But often, we create groups or subgroups that, when it comes right down to it, really exist for the brutal and childish purpose of making us feel that we belong *because* others are excluded. And the Church is not immune from being used for that purpose.

As you might guess, I know a little about being excluded because some people sometimes draw circles that exclude Japanese people. I also know a little about circles being drawn that have excluded me because I'm a woman.

Often these circles are invisible to the people drawing them, and the people excluded by them remain invisible to those within the circle. Several months ago, a woman who was serving as a Relief Society president from outside Utah was visiting in Salt Lake City and came in to see if she could talk to someone about a combination of personal and organizational problems. I was free, so I saw her. She was very intense and very troubled, pouring out her confusion and her frustrations. In the midst of this conversation, I saw Aileen Clyde, the second counselor in the general presidency, go past the door. She's a good listener, too, so I said to this sister, "Oh, let me have Sister Clyde come in, too. I know she has a real interest in some of these concerns."

Aileen willingly came in, met this sister, and sat down. And when she did, the sister picked up her chair and turned it away from me to face Sister Clyde, who is, like this woman, blond and Caucasian. Aileen's mouth dropped open and she started to say something. I made a comment to attract the woman's attention back to me. She glanced briefly at me, but turned back to Aileen and continued to talk, pouring out all of her frustrations. Aileen was getting more and more uncomfortable; and she finally started to move *her* chair over next to mine so that the woman would be facing both of us. I caught her eye and just shook my head a little. I could tell that this sister was so distraught and so consumed with her own worries that she really hadn't realized what she had done. But how revealing it was of the circles she drew in her own mind! What a lot of rules she carried around in her own mind about whom she could talk to, whom she could trust, whom she could share her burdens with.

Do we have secret lists of rules like that? Do we sometimes say to ourselves, "Oh, I don't want to go visiting teaching to *her!* She's never been married. What on earth would we have to talk about?" Or do we say, "I couldn't possibly work with *her* on a project. She's so wrapped up in those six children of hers that I don't think we have anything in common." Or, "Well, I guess she can come to our book group if she wants to, but we're all younger than she is and she's a widow besides. I think attending might just make her feel bad." Or, "Well, I'm sure she's very nice, but she's just eighteen. I can't imagine what interests we could possibly share."

What kind of circles are we drawing when we exclude anyone from any activity on the basis of their life circumstances?

I love Louise Plummer's retelling of the parable of the ant and the grasshopper. Louise is a prizewinning author of young adult fiction who came to the United States with her Dutch parents when she was young. She teaches writing at Brigham Young University and gave this wonderful talk on the ant and the grasshopper at a BYU Women's Conference a few years ago. She says:

> I first became acquainted with the story of the grasshopper and the ant as a young girl—not by reading Aesop's fable, but by seeing a Walt Disney cartoon. In the cartoon the grasshopper fiddles and sings and eats the leaves off trees while the ants are gathering food to store for the winter. The queen of ants warns him that he'd better prepare for winter too, but the grasshopper continues fiddling and singing. When winter comes, the grasshopper, blue from cold, can no longer play his fiddle. In desperation, he knocks on the tree where the ants live and begs them to let him in. The queen of ants gives her "I-told-you-so" speech and ends with, "So take your fiddle and"—there is a long pause—"and play." So the grasshopper earns the warmth and food of the ants by playing his fiddle.
>
> Aesop, in contrast, is not as kind to the grasshopper. When he comes begging for food, the ant merely tells him, "You sang through the summer; now you can dance through the winter."

Now, Louise grew up in an ant family as one of nine children.

> My mother kept the house and us immaculately. She knitted us sweaters and baked our bread. Dinner was ready each night at 5:30 on the nose. She taught me the correct principles of work. She forced me to wash woodwork, wax floors, and clean behind the toilet. . . . I love to open her linen closet and see the neatly folded sheets and pillow cases, color-coordinated, meticulously stacked. I like to stand in front of the year's supply in her dust-free basement and admire the rows of preserves, of laundry soap, of peanut butter, and of polyunsaturated oils. I like to see her white—really white—laundry blowing on the clothesline. I like to ask her for the kinds of things that I can never find in my own house—like the negative of a picture taken twenty years ago or a darning needle. She always knows where such things are located.

But if Louise's mother is an ant, Louise is definitely a grasshopper: "I dance in elevators," she admits cheerfully.

The second the door closes, I begin tap dancing and flinging my arms wildly about. I make faces and stick my tongue out at the hidden cameras I believe exist in every elevator. When the doors open, I stop short and stare with what I hope is a bored elevator look into the open hallway ahead.

. . . It takes me a full day to dismantle my Christmas tree because I dress up in the decorations. I wrap the gold tinsel around my head like a turban. I make a shawl for my neck from glass beads and paper chains. I have a special pair of vampy red high heels that I wear only on the day I undecorate the tree. Red glass balls hang from my ears. I sing . . . "New York, New York—if you can make it there, you'll make it anywhere." . . .

I have never prepared for winter or the Apocalypse. I do have two thousand pounds of wheat that I hope never to eat and a box of chocolate chips that won't last through next week. Last summer I tried to bottle some peaches—the cold pack method—just to see if I could do it. I bottled three jars full. They sit in my freezer like museum pieces.

If you're an ant, what do you do with grasshoppers? Louise says something that is very sad: "I always wondered if there was room in a family of ants for a grasshopper, room in a community of ants for a grasshopper, or room in a church of ants for a grasshopper." What do you think? Is there? God made both ants and grasshoppers and gave them their own spaces and their own way of being. God thinks there's room enough in his world for ants and grasshoppers. He didn't tell the grasshoppers to behave like ants nor the ants like grasshoppers. He probably gave both of them the same commands—to bring forth after their kind. We know that he looked upon the creeping things of the earth—which include both ants and grasshoppers—and "saw that it was good" (Genesis 1:25). So why is it sometimes hard for ants to welcome grasshoppers or hard for grasshoppers to respect the contributions of ants?

Louise gives us an example of how ants and grasshoppers can share the same space.

I would like to rewrite the ending of "The Grasshopper and the Ants" like this: It is winter, and the grasshopper is walking in the snow, talking to herself and answering herself. She wears a yellow slicker over her sweater because she can't find her parka (which is buried in the debris under her bed). Because she was out of groceries this morning, she is eating a brownie with a car- ton of milk bought at the 7-Eleven which, thank heaven, is open 365 days a year. The door in the tree where the ants live swings open. The queen ant appears and says to the grasshopper, "We are bored to death. Won't you tell us a story or at least a good joke? Our teenagers are driving us crazy; maybe you would write them a play to perform, or just a roadshow? Do you have any ideas for a daddy-daughter party?"

The grasshopper replies that she has ideas for all of them. So the ant invites her in and seats her at a spotless kitchen table with pencil and paper, and the grasshopper writes the roadshow. The ant feeds her guest a slice of homemade bread, fresh from the oven, and a glass of freshly squeezed orange juice. "How do you get all of these ideas?" she asks the grasshopper.

"They come to me," says the grasshopper, "while I am taking long hot baths."

This is a happy ending for both the creative grasshopper and the hardworking ant. But Louise has one other message for us:

> "What about works?" someone may ask. "Don't ants work *harder* than grasshoppers?"
>
> No. Grasshoppers work *differently* from ants.[1]

I think this is very important. Differences are just that—dif- ferences. If we think of them as differences to be fixed, then they become weapons with which we wound each other. If we think of them as delightful, then they become a bouquet of bright blossoms.

Maybe there are ways that ants and grasshoppers can't work together—but there are usually parts of the same project where they can cooperate or times when the same project needs the talents of both. When we know what our differences and similar- ities are, then we can capitalize on them happily. Do you know what you like to do at church? What kind of service nourishes your soul? What kinds of contributions do you want to make?

Of course you do. And I'll bet you know what makes you absolutely bored or terribly anxious, too. Knowledge of yourself is the strongest foundation for acceptance and tolerance. When you know about your own differences and value them, then you can see the personal preferences, and idiosyncrasies, and, yes, downright eccentricities and irritating qualities of others and say, "Well, of course. She's different in her way, just as I'm different in mine. There are probably things I do that drive her crazy, too."

Whose job is it to recognize these differences? Whose job is inclusion? It's yours! It's mine! This is a job for every sister in the Relief Society. It's not just a job for the leaders or the teachers. It's not just a job for the visiting teachers. Make accepting differences *your* job.

Lighten up! It's no big deal. You can smile and say hello. You can ask how someone is doing. You can listen when someone shares an experience. You can tell someone you're glad to see her. You can ask someone to help you. Now, that's not so hard, is it?

Dealing with Differences

It's obvious that the Lord doesn't mind differences. He sent us here just the way we are, each of us with our own needs, our own abilities, our own desires for righteousness, and our own set of obstacles to overcome. Sometimes we worry that others are different. We are uncomfortable when they surprise us. We don't know how to act when someone says something different or acts differently. I think we should all lighten up. Our charge from the Lord is to *bear* one another's burdens, not to *increase* one another's burdens. We don't need to increase our own burdens either.

You may not like someone else's differences. You may not even like your own. You may be using yourself as a punching bag because you're not married. You may be a widow and feeling uncomfortable around women who still have their companions.

The first party I went to after Ed's death was a general board party where we were saying good-bye to the outgoing Young Women presidency. No one could be a closer circle of sisters. But did I feel uncomfortable and out of place? You bet I did. It was terrible! If you are healthy, you may feel nervous around women who are ill. You may be infertile and unable to relate to the young mother who is struggling with preschoolers. You may be employed outside of the home but feel that women are looking judgmentally at you every time someone talks about the responsibilities of motherhood.

Well, there are dozens of circumstances, personality traits, and preferences that create differences. The differences are real. They are unavoidable, and they are okay. Judging yourself and judging others because of them is *not* okay. Judging is such an important job that God the Father reserves it to his Son for the last day—and promises even then that Jesus will be our advocate. You don't have to judge another. You don't even have to judge yourself. Just do your best. We need diversity. We need differences. We need both grasshoppers and ants. Remember, the way of love is to draw a circle that includes, not one that excludes. Differences are okay. If we can lighten up about them we'll find that differences are delicious and delightful, not dangerous and damaging!

When You Feel Excluded

But what should we do when we feel excluded? The Savior's way is to turn quickly away from being offended and angry. As non-Caucasians, Ed and I were people who showed our differences in our faces. We became something of experts on what to do when we felt excluded, and we began from our love for the gospel and our trust that it would work. We knew that anger and resentment would poison our lives and make it impossible for us to live the gospel.

Let me give you some stories about our experience. You may know that I was the first non-Caucasian called to serve on any general board. It was Florence Jacobsen, general president of the YWMIA, who had me called to that board. At that time, no woman *or* man who was not Caucasian had been called to serve on any auxiliary board. No non-Caucasian had ever served as a mission president, a temple president, a Regional Representative or a General Authority. We had lived in Salt Lake City since 1951. I was working as the first exchange teacher in Uintah School and Ed was completing his Master's of Social Work degree at the University of Utah. People stared at us when we went shopping. People stared at us in the temple. A Japanese person could not be sealed to a Caucasian in the Salt Lake Temple at that time because of state law. We could not buy life insurance and could not insure our cars. People on the street saw our Japanese faces and sometimes reacted to them with feelings we could tell had their origin in losses during World War II.

We knew that arguing would not solve anything. We simply tried to behave like good neighbors, like good Americans, like good Christians. For example, when we were renting apartments, Ed, who grew up in Hawaiian sunshine like me, quietly got up on winter mornings and shoveled snow off the driveway and the sidewalks. When we moved out of an apartment, we always left it spotless. We always spoke first to neighbors, since we knew that sometimes they weren't even sure if we spoke English. And if they didn't speak back, we still smiled and said hello the next time we saw them.

We had difficulty buying a home and were very grateful when Grant Burns, Ed's companion on a regional mission to the Japanese people of Salt Lake City, sold us a lot he owned. Just recently Grant and his wife came to visit us. We thanked him for his help in selling us the lot. Then he said, "I've never told you this, but I received two calls from people in the neighborhood. They asked me why I sold the lot to 'those Japanese people.' I didn't respond in any way except to ask them to call me a year from now and tell me how they felt. Both of them did call, a year to the day, and said, 'We're glad to have the Okazakis as neighbors.' "

But you get the point. Ed and I and our boys have spent a big chunk of our lives being different. There have been many, many occasions when Ed and I could have taken offense. In fact, we have often said to each other, "If we were going to lose our testimonies, it would have been here in Zion." But we didn't lose our testimonies. We understood that we had the power to choose, and we had already chosen. We had chosen the gospel over the religion of our families, we had chosen each other over the voices that warned about a marriage of mixed religions. We had chosen the mainland over the familiarity and comforts of our home island. We had chosen the way of the Savior over the way of the world. We knew we were tougher than our problems. I have three little mottos that I sometimes repeat to myself during interesting situations like these:

First: If both of us thought alike, one of us would not be necessary.

Second, I may be the first Japanese (or woman or Mormon or widow) in this setting, but I'm going to do my best to ensure that I won't be the last.

Third—and this is really a prayer: Help, Father. I have a message they may not have heard before. How can I say it so they can hear it?

Most people will try to understand if you make these efforts; but recognize that there will be people who won't want you there, who won't hear what you say, who will misunderstand you, sometimes on purpose. If you feel excluded, recognize that it may not be intentional. But whether the offense is intentional or not, your job is still the same. I implore you: Please forgive them quickly so that no negative thoughts will hold *you* back or make it harder for them to change. If you don't forgive a person who has offended you, you create a negative relationship that becomes a second burden on top of the original problem. I do not ask you to pretend that these wounds did not happen. I do not ask you to deny your pain. But I do ask you not to be a martyr.

I also ask you something else. If you experience the pain of exclusion at church from someone who is frightened at your difference, please don't leave. Don't become inactive. You may think you are voting with your feet, that you are making a statement by leaving. You are, but your absence may be welcomed and encouraged by those who don't understand or value you. They see your diversity as a problem to be fixed, as a flaw to be corrected or erased. If you are gone, they don't have to deal with you any more. I want you to know that your diversity is a more valuable statement. Elder Neal A. Maxwell talks about "saintly sisters, . . . women of light" who are "idealists without illusions."[2] I'm asking you to be idealists without illusions, to dig deep for the strength, the compassion, and the toughness you need to find your own way.

Please stay. Please be a bridge builder. You may feel marginalized, pushed to the edge, invisible, unwanted, not valuable. I tell you that you are visible, are wanted, are valuable. I love you. We need each other's support. We need each other's prayers.

Ed and I, over the course of our lives, have found that a very helpful approach to take is to concentrate on the job that needs to be done. A good deed or a necessary task never complains because the "wrong person" does it. From the task's perspective, the only thing that is important is getting it done. At Jesus' time, the Jews and the Samaritans had not spoken to each other in kindness for hundreds of years. They despised each other. The Jews considered the Samaritans unworthy to worship in the temple, barely fit to be human beings. But when the Jewish man who fell among thieves was lying in pain by the road into Jericho, did he complain that bandages on his wounds were too Samaritan? That the donkey on which he was lifted had an inappropriate genealogy? That the money that paid for his room and care at the inn had not been properly tithed? I doubt it very, very much. That Samaritan asked the right questions. He asked, "What does this man need?"

Do we sometimes catch ourselves in our own culture drawing circles of things that only men can do, only women can do? I've never heard a dish complain because a man washed it instead of a woman. I remember that when I was on the Primary

General Board a stake Primary president told me that the nursery leader in one of the wards was a man. It was pretty obvious
that he knew what he was doing, she said. He hugged every
child, sat on the floor with them, held them on his lap, talked
quietly to them, laughed with them, and looked them straight
in the eyes when they were talking. She loved being there,
watching him with the children.

"How long have you had this calling?" she asked.

"Three years," he said.

"Oh," she said. "And what was your calling before?"

"I was the bishop," he said.

I just loved it! And I remember feeling so proud of one of
our former missionaries who asked to be released from the stake
high council so that he could teach his son's Primary class.
Doesn't it say something that these examples are rare enough
that we pick them out and hold them up? Is there a lesson here
for us? Do we fall into the hierarchical trap? Do we make little
models in our minds and say, "Oh, X job is much more important than Y job. Therefore, the person who has X assignment is
a more important person than Y." Well, what happens when we
think like that? We equate our worth with our status. Then we
sometimes feel terribly unhappy and rejected if we don't get a
glamorous calling in the Church. Sometimes we also feel terribly depressed and sad when we're released from a calling.

Some time ago, my husband and I took an elderly friend to a
performance at BYU. We hadn't made ticket reservations ahead
of time; and the girl at the ticket window apologetically said,
"I'm sorry, but we only have tickets left on the top three rows. Is
that all right?"

"Of course that's fine," we told her. We took the tickets and
were moving away when another girl came up. She looked at
me, then whispered something to the girl at the ticket counter.
The ticket-seller came hurriedly after us and said, "Please let me
exchange those tickets for some tickets down front." She was
flustered and apologetic, and it was pretty obvious that the second girl had told her I was in the Relief Society General Presidency.

She was very young, obviously a student and obviously just following directions. We didn't want to make her feel bad, so we simply just thanked her and didn't make a fuss, especially since there weren't other people waiting to buy tickets. But I felt a little heartsore even as we enjoyed the performance from those excellent seats. I had discovered another circle, one that said, "You're special because of your calling." Well, this calling came and this calling will go. I don't like being treated as though I *am* the calling. I don't think most people do.

I want to ask you another question. After Jesus got up off his knees from washing the dusty, muddy feet of his disciples, what do you think *he* would have said about things like this? You know perfectly well what he would have said. It's exactly what he *did* say: "He [or she] that is greatest among you shall be your servant" (Matthew 23:11). And Peter, in his vision of the gospel net, learned that he had been drawing exclusionary circles and, with his new insight, joyously exclaimed: "Of a truth I perceive that God is no respecter of persons: but in every nation [the individual] that feareth him, and worketh righteousness, is accepted with him" (Acts 10:34–35).

As somebody who is newly single in a married church, I know that every single person has sat in some meeting and felt invisible. At some point, something in a program has simply erased the single people present, or a speaker has created a marital circle that excludes everyone not in it. It's so heartbreakingly easy to exclude. How often do elderly people feel excluded? How often do converts feel excluded? How often do single men feel excluded by lesson after lesson after lesson that talks about family responsibilities? How often does ward or stake leadership look like a very closed circle that excludes women?

I once heard a Regional Representative addressing a ward conference. The congregation consisted of men, women, and children; and not necessarily in equal numbers either! He was talking about the importance of living the gospel and was saying things like, "You need to fast and pray for answers to your problems. You need to study the scriptures and come to your meetings." And then he said, "You need to help your wives and

children understand the gospel." Bang! I'd thought he was talking to *all* of us and then suddenly, just like that, I wasn't there
anymore. He'd erased me and he'd erased our two teenage boys.
The only person he saw sitting on our row was Ed. The only
person in our family who counted to him was Ed.

I think the same thing happens to poor people in a generally
affluent church. I know it happens to childless men on Father's
Day and it *really* happens to childless women on Mother's Day. I
heard a young mother speak once at a Mother's Day program.
She was pregnant with her third child in five years; and the
family was struggling financially, but she quoted President Benson's 1987 talk very firmly and announced, "You women who
are out of the home working instead of having children, you'd
just better think about what you should be doing instead." Now,
Ed and I would have welcomed every child who came to our
home; but we had only two sons. It had been more than twenty
years since a miscarriage ended our last hope for a third child,
and I *still* flinched when she said that. And sitting not more
than three rows away in one direction and four rows away in another direction were two young couples who I know were going
through fertility workups. One of them had already had two
surgeries. How must they have felt?

I hear a lot of stories about the pain caused women by men
in the Church—not so much because of the different assignments that result from the priesthood but because of the different status attached to priesthood assignments versus women's
assignments. I have a book I just love called *Children's Letters to
God.* Children put their finger squarely on sometimes prickly
truths that we adults are pretty good about shying away from or
covering up. One of these letters reads: "Dear God, Are boys
better than girls? I know you are one but try to be fair. [Signed]
Sylvia." Can we be fair? I think we have to try.

I got a letter a few weeks ago from a member of a Relief Society presidency in England asking me how she could work with
her elders quorum president. "He doesn't listen to me," she said.
"In our meetings, he never asks for my opinion or asks what information I have about a situation. He just gives me orders." I

thought, "How do we help men and women in this Church to understand that we need to work together in a partnership? How do we get people to focus on service—on what's best for the members being served—instead of on giving orders *or* taking orders?" I don't know what advice you would have given her; but the fact that she wrote to me, on the other side of the world, hoping I could take care of a problem that was happening in her own ward, indicated to me that we need help in negotiating conflicts on a very local level, not a global one. If what she needed was my encouragement and support, I could certainly give her that. But the person who needed to talk to that elders quorum president was the person who was suffering because of his behavior—and that was the Relief Society president.

Now, I'm not so naive as to think that there are no problems in the Church. But I think most people can hear a message that says: "When you give me orders, I feel put down, and then I feel resentful of feeling like that. We need to find a way to work together better. Will you help?" That Regional Representative I mentioned wasn't evil, he was insensitive. That young pregnant woman on the Mother's Day program may have been a little defensive; she was doing something so hard that she had to be sure she was right and assumed all of the other women in the ward were in her situation. I think it was mostly ignorance. That doesn't lessen the pain, but it *does* allow for forgiveness and it does mean that change is possible.

We each grow up in a culture and in overlapping spheres of different cultures. There's the culture of our home. There's the culture of our immediate environment. There's our larger social culture. If we belong to a racial or ethnic minority, there's the overlay of still another culture. If you're a convert in the LDS church, you're aware of two separate religious cultures, but the gospel culture is the one that will ultimately infuse, replace, and transform every human culture on the earth. Are we trying to move into that gospel culture already, or are we putting our energy into preserving one of these old cultural forms like hierarchy and gender and youth and wealth that will be swept away when the Savior comes again?

The Book of Mormon tells us that the Savior "inviteth . . . all to come unto him and partake of his goodness; and he denieth none that come unto him, black and white, bond and free, male and female; . . . and all are alike unto God" (2 Nephi 26:33). If that's the ultimate destination we want, then we cannot afford to indulge ourselves in excluding people that the Savior is trying hard to include.

Working on Inclusiveness

Special interest groups are wonderful. Grasshoppers have them. Ants have them. Create them. Enjoy them. But remember that the *Church* is for everybody. More particularly, Relief Society is for anyone who is eighteen, female, and present. Within that sisterhood, every woman belongs. What can *you* do to contribute to that sense of belonging?

We in the presidency have a special concern about our eighteen-year-old women. Since they come in birthday by birthday, they don't even have the extra bit of confidence they'd get from arriving with a best friend. There's a big difference between eighteen and sixty-six. I'm sixty-six now and I can still remember what it was like when I was eighteen. I was in college and I joined Relief Society, paid my dues, and taught the theology lessons. I felt totally accepted. I knew this was Christ's church and that associating with the sisters was exactly what Jesus wanted me to do. Besides that, I'd been attending Relief Society with the Hawaiian sisters in my home village of Mahukona ever since I was an eleven-year-old investigator. Those are precious experiences for me to remember. After college when I was working during the day, I couldn't go to Relief Society. In fact, I didn't attend Relief Society again until the second-session Relief Societies began when I was a principal in Denver. My circumstances excluded that kind of participation. For a large part of my life, Relief Society was not a place I belonged, except in my heart.

Maybe you have some moments of feeling that Relief Society

is not a place where you belong? Or you feel marginal enough in your own belonging that you're not sure how to make someone else feel welcome? Sometimes we feel shy in new situations. Sometimes we don't know what to say or how to act. Sometimes when we meet a stranger, we want to let someone else do the talking. Well, Ed and I didn't usually feel we could wait that long to make friends.

When we moved from Colorado back to Utah in 1988, we bought a home in Wasatch Fifth Ward. We didn't sit on the back row hoping members of the ward would introduce themselves to us. We moved in on a Thursday and spent Friday and Saturday unpacking. When we saw teenagers in the yard of the house across the street, we walked over, introduced ourselves, and asked the three golden questions: "Where's the ward? What time is church? Who's the bishop?" Ed and I were there at church early. We walked in, shaking hands and introducing ourselves to everyone we saw. By the time we got to the chapel, we had twenty or thirty new acquaintances. We introduced ourselves to the bishop and explained our circumstances. We introduced ourselves in class.

Giving fortune cookies was something of a trademark with Ed, something he'd done ever since we'd lived in Denver. As soon as he found a place to buy them wholesale in Salt Lake City, he was in business! We visited all our neighbors. Ed took packets to every teenager in the ward who gave a talk or sang a song. We had our neighbors over to dinner. At Ed's funeral in April, our bishop was still shaking his head. He said:

> Ed and Chieko didn't wait for us to come to them. They came to us. Ed crossed the fence lines and the invisible lines of age, gender, and religion until he had met everyone in the neighborhood. Ed was able to get more mileage out of a tiny bag of fortune cookies than the combined empires of Asia realized with gunpowder. They immediately became "Ed and Chieko" to all of the children of the neighborhood. When my own grandchildren would come to visit, they would race up the stairs and say, "Hi, Grandma. Hi, Grandpa. Can we go see Ed and Chieko?" Ed would give them fortune cookies, then take them out to the front

yard where he had a goodly supply of snails and would help them catch snails and put them in a jar to bring home.

Not everyone could do what we did or would feel comfortable doing it. But having been excluded ourselves, we've learned to take extraordinary measures to include others. What can you do? If you are waiting to be included, think about some steps you can take to put yourself at the center of a circle, a circle of inclusion. You can do this at any age—eighteen or eighty—and in any circumstances. Restrictions are only in your mind.

Perhaps you think you have nothing to give. Others seem so self-sufficient. They seem to have nothing you could share, have no points in common with you, or even are so busy giving service to others that they would be astonished if you offered service to them. Don't forget that the act of service is usually only a vehicle for carrying a feeling of love. Love is the important part. Service per se can be routine, even unfeeling; but love never is, and nobody can ever have too much love. Carolyn Rasmus, the dedicated and hard-working administrative assistant to the Young Women General Presidency, tells a wonderful story about how, as a single woman, she drew a circle of loving inclusions.

My friend Kathryn and I live together. We had planned to see *Driving Miss Daisy* on the last day of our vacations. Everyone was talking about that movie and . . . we wanted to see it. Besides going to movies, one of the things I love to do when I have time off work is to bake bread. I got carried away; that afternoon I baked eight loaves. . . . We had about thirty minutes before we were to leave for the movie. I said to Kathy, "It's going to take us a long time to eat eight loaves of bread. Why don't we take one over to [leave our neighbor]?" This was during the heated debate in the state legislature about teachers' salaries. Our . . . neighbor . . . was . . . the focus of a lot of controversy. . . . We rang the doorbell; [our neighbor] came to the door. As we handed her the bread, she started to cry. She was home alone and had been for several days and nights. She said to us, "*Please* come in." I wondered what we would talk about, but I needn't have—all we had to do was listen.

When we left we felt so good we said, "Let's give away an-other loaf of bread. . . ." We debated about going to our next-door neighbors because only two days before their son had been con-victed of sexually molesting children and was in the state prison. What would we say to his parents? We didn't know. . . . The father came to the door and said, "Please, *please* come in. Nobody has talked to us. We've got to talk to somebody." We listened for more than an hour to a mother and father, whose hearts were breaking, tell us about their son. When we got ready to leave, they hugged us. As we returned home Kathy said, "We missed the second showing, but who cares!"[3]

Carolyn and Kathy inspire me. They drew circles of love—not because they had two loaves of bread to give away but be-cause they had hearts that were willing to listen without judging and the time to give to someone else. Every woman in the Church has the same talent, capability, and power. We all have the ability to include.

The Savior's Love

When we love and include others, we are doing what the Savior wants us to do. We are doing what he does for us. With all my heart I testify that our own ability to love comes from Jesus Christ. Our Savior is with us. He is close beside us. He is not a theological abstraction. He is not a factor in a power equa-tion. He is a person who loves us, who serves us, who died for us. According to the baptismal covenant that we renew each time we partake of the sacrament, we take the name of Christ upon us. We become Christians. We remember Christ. We represent Christ. And in turn he promises that we will always have his Spirit with us. Since Ed's death I have experienced loneliness in ways I could not even have imagined, and during those moments of bitter sorrow and need I have clung to the promise of the sacrament prayer. I have needed that promised companionship. And I know that I have received it. I understand more of what it means to take the name of Christ upon us. Our individual identities become modified by the identity of Christ. He becomes our friend. We know him. When we speak to someone, we do it the way Jesus would have done it. Our hearts are centered on Christ. In him, the scriptures tell us, we live and move and have our being.

When I read the scriptures, I get a sense of the overwhelming love of the Savior and the Father for us. The Saints are a treasure, jewels, a chosen people to them. In the Doctrine and Covenants the Savior tells Joseph Smith: "They shall be mine in that day when I shall come to make up my jewels" (D&C 101:3). "Ye are my friends" (D&C 84:63). "Lift up your hearts and be glad, for I am in your midst, and am your advocate with the Father; and it is his good will to give you the kingdom" (D&C 29:5). In Deuteronomy, Moses tells the people that the Lord "set his love upon you" and "chose you" (Deuteronomy 7:6–7).

How does it make you feel to hear scriptures like these? I tingle and feel warm inside. I feel joy. I feel wonder. I feel humility. And most of all, I feel a desire to be more like Christ, to know him better, to follow him better. Ed has always been the best Christian I know. He had been Christ's all of his life—first as a Congregationalist and then as a Mormon. Since his death, I know that he is with the Savior and that the Spirit of the Savior is with me and my sons. We sorrowed greatly and still do, but we can bear it. We are enclosed within the loving circle of the Savior's arms.

I ask that we support one another as members of the Church, both men and women, and particularly that we sisters support each other. Let us reach out to each other with tenderness, and good humor, and service. Reach out especially to the women who have chosen to absent themselves from this circle of sisterhood. Reach out to women in the community, to the men with whom we live and work, to the children who are learning about life. Draw them into your circle of love. Recognize and cherish the diversity of others. Go beyond acceptance to love.

The Apostle Paul has a beautiful and powerful description of how we should live together in our wards. This is a modern translation of Ephesians 4:2–7.

Be completely humble and gentle; be patient, bearing with one another in love. Make every effort to keep the unity of the Spirit through the bond of peace. There is one body and one Spirit—just as you were called to one hope when you were called—one Lord, one faith, one baptism, one God and Father of all, who is over all and through all and in all. But to *each one* of us grace has been given as Christ apportioned it. (The Holy Bible, New International Version, 1981, italics added; hereafter cited as NIV.)

Paul then explains that the different offices of the Church have been given "to prepare God's people for works of service, so that the body of Christ may be built up until we all reach unity in the faith and in the knowledge of the Son of God and become mature, attaining to the whole measure of the fullness of Christ" (NIV, Ephesians 4:12–13).

Conclusion

I testify to you that our differences are strengths, not problems to be fixed. If you have experienced the pain of being excluded, let yours be the heart that sees the hunger of others to be included. Let yours be the words of sensitivity and kindness that include. Let yours be the voice of courage, lifted in asking thoughtful questions when insensitivity or limitation or ignorance would exclude. And let yours be the blessing promised by Paul: "Speaking the truth in love, we will in all things grow up into him who is the Head, that is, Christ. From him the whole body, joined and held together by every supporting ligament, grows and builds itself up into love, as each part does its work." (NIV, Ephesians 4:15–16.)

Notes

1. Louise Plummer, "Thoughts of a Grasshopper," in *A Heritage of Faith: Talks Selected from the BYU Women's Conferences,* edited by Mary E. Stovall and Carol Cornwall Madsen, (Salt Lake City: Deseret Book Company, 1988), pp. 185–91, italics added. Used by permission.

2. Neal A. Maxwell, "Women of Faith," in *As Women of Faith: Talks Selected from the BYU Women's Conferences*, edited by Mary E. Stovall and Carol Cornwall Madsen (Salt Lake City: Deseret Book Company, 1989), p. 21.

3. Carolyn J. Rasmus, speaking in the jointly delivered address, "To Cheer and Bless in Humanity's Name," by Ardeth G. Kapp and Carolyn J. Rasmus. In *Women and the Power Within: To See Life Steadily and See It Whole*, edited by Dawn Hall Anderson and Marie Cornwall (Salt Lake City: Deseret Book Company, 1991), p. 39. Used by permission.

PART TWO

Changes and Choices

5

Asking Better Questions

*D*uring 1992, as the Relief Society celebrated its 150th birthday, we Mormon women celebrated our shared past and looked to the future. Today I want to look into that past with you, then look ahead into our future. There's a real skill involved in drawing on the past without being bogged down by the past. And visualizing a future and moving into it is another very important skill. Sometimes we feel that this process happens to us. I feel that it's a process we can cooperate with, control to some extent, and enjoy while we're doing it. My profound belief is that we see what we expect to see. The questions we ask shape the answers we get. So what do we expect to see? And what kind of questions are we asking?

As I look into my past, I find that my enjoyment of the process of life really depended on the questions I was asking at that stage. At age fifteen, I spent the eighth of December—the

This address was presented at the Mount Vernon Washington Stake women's meeting, 8 February 1992.

day after Pearl Harbor—standing over the outdoor incinerator with my mother, stuffing into it everything in the house we could find that had come from Japan, looking anxiously over our shoulders down our little road and not knowing which to dread most—American soldiers or Japanese soldiers. What questions do you think I was asking about my future then? There's a big difference between a question like, "How can I hide? Where can I escape?" and a question like, "How can I make the best of this situation?" The fear could have lasted forever, but it didn't.

With my family, I decided that rather than hiding out for the duration of the war I should work as hard as I could to get an education. I had wanted to be a teacher ever since I'd been in the sixth grade, and my parents wanted more for me than plantation life. So despite the real uncertainty and fearfulness of our situation, we stayed focused on that goal. Our little village had no high school; and with gasoline rationing, there were no school buses to take the teenagers to Honomakau, the nearest town with a high school. Going on to high school, then, meant leaving my family and working as a cook and maid for a family eleven miles away. And that's what we decided I would do.

Now, World War II was very important, a cataclysmic event of global importance, shattering to individuals and families all around the world. But I did not spend those war years focused on the war. Of course, I felt how desperately important it was for the United States to win the war. My own feelings of patriotism were deep and strong. We were so conscious of the war effort. We took the fastest possible showers to save the kerosene used to heat the water. We didn't turn the lights on as long as there was enough daylight to see what we were doing. We were conscientious about observing the rationing regulations. With the other students, I spent half of every day working in the school's victory garden. I participated in the drives to collect tin foil and scrap metal.

But in the midst of this public turmoil, I had a private goal. I wanted to become a teacher. And that was the question I asked myself steadfastly and continually throughout those years: "What can I do to help me reach my goal of being a teacher?"

It was amazing how clear things became as a result of that goal. It was never easy to leave my family after being with them for a few hours or a few days. It was never easy to do all of the work I had to do for my employers plus my own school work. I had to deal with fear, loneliness, and overwhelming feelings of inadequacy for my tasks. But instead of focusing on these feelings I focused on my goal and found myself leaving fear behind me.

Now, I didn't consciously do all of this. I didn't even understand it all on a conscious level. But I could *feel* what I was doing. And when I was just seventeen I had one of the most wonderful rewards for these efforts that could be imagined. Benjamin Wist, the dean of the Teachers College at the University of Hawaii, came to visit our high school. In the afternoon the teachers held a tea for him, and I was invited to attend and help serve. He talked kindly to all of the teachers in the room and then looked at me.

"And what grade do you teach?" he asked.

I stared back at him in astonished delight. "Do I look like a teacher?" I exclaimed.

"Yes, you do," he responded.

I felt as if I had just been crowned queen. "Thank you very much," I said proudly. "I want to be a teacher, and next year I hope to be entering your college."

He looked at me keenly and smiled kindly. "I will remember you," he said. And he did.

How I cherished that compliment! I realize now that he was seeing, manifested on the outside, the inner vision of myself that I had nurtured. He did not see a frightened third-generation Japanese-American girl. He did not even see a *potential* teacher. He saw a teacher!

The point I'm making is that I asked questions about myself and what I expected my life to be that were empowering, not limiting. Living was a process I enjoyed, not a mysterious process that baffled and frightened me. When we remember the power of asking clear questions about our future, then we can see the future rearrange itself to answer those questions.

This process works not only for individuals but also for

institutions. When we look at the past and the future together, we find answers collectively so that we share the enjoyment of life. For instance, we're all members of the Relief Society. When you think of the great causes and great achievements of the Relief Society, both in the past and in the present, we think of things like:

— helping with the Nauvoo Temple by supplying clothing for the workers
— the visiting teaching program, both historically and now, providing compassionate service
— the grain storage program
— manufacturing silk
— Relief Society cooperative stores
— medical training and the creation and support of women's hospitals
— building and maintaining their own Relief Society halls
— organizing as branches of the American Red Cross during World War I and World War II to assist in a major way with war support and relief
— undertaking many social betterment projects during the 1910s and 1920s, including well-baby care, inoculations, playgrounds for children, and recreational facilities for youth
— building the Relief Society Building
— becoming professionally trained social service workers or paraprofessionals during the 1920s and 1930s to develop much of the program that later became the Welfare Program and LDS Social Services
— compassionate service in a variety of traditional ways, including visiting teaching
— many community service projects
— the literacy effort

That's quite an impressive list, isn't it? All of these accomplishments are fine and generous achievements, but I have a strong sense that the most important accomplishment isn't organizational at all. In my opinion, one of the most important processes of the Relief Society is not so much to change the world out there but to change the world in our heart. One of the greatest blessings of Relief Society work is that it will empower us as individual women. If I were to have a goal for the Relief Society it might be to help each of us three million women on the Relief Society rolls to become powerful women—powerful in the gospel sense. I want us to be Latter-day Saint women who can think creatively about ways to solve our own problems, express ourselves effectively, find ways to apply gospel principles in our lives, feel our identity as daughters of God, and make wise choices for ourselves and our children—to be holy women, loving women, saintly women, sisters of Christ. If we all drew on the miraculous power of the Savior and his love to transform lives, don't you think we could make a good start right where we are?

We think of the sesquicentennial as an event—a party, a celebration. Let's also think of it as a process, a process that has lasted over 150 years so far, and one that will continue into the future. I felt impressed to return to President Kimball's addresses in 1979, the year before the Church's sesquicentennial. I asked myself, "What message did he give the whole Church on the eve of that important event?" He issued a quiet challenge that has rung in my heart ever since. Sometimes there's only the faintest reverberation, like a set of chimes barely tinkling if a heavy truck goes by on the street. Sometimes it rings so powerfully that I can feel its strokes in my very bones. Listen to what he said—and where he said "Church," think "Relief Society" and where he said "individual member," think "me":

This impression weighs upon me—that the Church is at a point in its growth and maturity when we are at last ready to move forward in a major way. Some decisions have been made and others [are] pending, which will clear the way, organizationally. But the basic decisions needed for us to move forward, as a people, must be made by the individual members of the Church. The major strides which must be made by the Church will follow upon the major strides to be made by us as individuals.

Doesn't that thrill you and make you catch your breath? It does me! Then he continued:

> Seemingly small efforts in the life of each member could do so much to move the Church forward as never before. . . .
>
> Are we ready, brothers and sisters, to do these seemingly small things out of which great blessings will proceed? I think we are. I believe the Lord's church is on the verge of an upsurge in spirituality. Our individual spiritual growth is the key to major numerical growth in the kingdom. The Church is ready to accomplish these things now which it could not have done just a few years ago. So also, we are ready as members. . . .
>
> Let us not shrink from the next steps in our spiritual growth. . . . Let us trust the Lord and take the next steps in our individual lives.

Are we asking ourselves certain questions right now—perhaps, "What did President Kimball have in mind? What are these simple steps that he said we can take?" If we heard him say these things in 1979, weren't we burning with curiosity to know what simple individual progress each one of us could make that would move the Church forward in this way? I wish I knew how many women have joined the Church since April 1979. I suspect that at least some of them came into the Church because they knew and admired a Mormon woman, man, youth, or child. That's one of the simple steps President Kimball said we could take—to share the gospel with others.

What were some of the other things he asked us to do? In the same address I just quoted he asked us to keep a journal. Will that increase our spirituality? It certainly will. I don't know very many people who, when they examine their lives, do not find powerful evidence in them of the love of God. President Kimball asked us to serve the dead by performing their endowments in the temple. He asked us to give "a few more minutes of individual attention each month" to "our spouses and children."

He asked us not to let sin immobilize us or hamper us with guilt. He asked us to "stretch just a little bit more in service" and not to be "shy about letting [our] lights shine." He asked us to make our homes "a place where we love to be, a place of listening and learning, a place where each member can find mutual love, support, appreciation, and encouragement." He promised us: "We will move faster if we hurry less. We will make more real progress if we focus on the fundamentals." He wanted us to know Christ better and to feed his sheep.[1]

Isn't that wonderful? These are not new things. They are not hard things. We're probably already doing many of them. And it's these simple, familiar things that will transform the Church and move it to a completely new plateau! It's a simple process that we can individually set in motion. And we can enjoy that process!

President Kimball gave this talk in the spring of 1979. In the fall of that year he had a message for the women of the Church at the women's fireside preceding October general conference. The counsel he had given in the spring was to the whole Church—men, women, children, families, couples, and singles. But in the fall he told us, the women, how to implement this mighty individual change that would transform the Church:

> Much of the major growth that is coming to the Church in the last days will come because many of the good women of the world (in whom there is often such an inner sense of spirituality) will be drawn to the Church in large numbers. This will happen to the degree that the women of the Church reflect righteousness and articulateness in their lives and to the degree that the women of the Church are seen as distinct and different—in happy ways— from the women of the world. . . .
> . . . Female exemplars of the Church will be a significant force in both the numerical and the spiritual growth of the Church in the last days.

Elder Ballard quoted this same promise at the general women's meeting in September 1991. I truly believe this promise: that individual righteousness is the key to a real transformation in the Church. I consider these two talks to be scripture to us. What President Kimball said to the whole Church on the eve of its 150th anniversary is a promise that I think applied equally well to the Relief Society on the eve of *its* 150th anniversary. I searched President Kimball's talk again for those simple things that we can do individually, to transform first our lives, then to transform the Church.

I found, again, the kind of counsel we would have expected. He asked us to become "sister scriptorians—whether [we] are single or married, young or old, widowed or living in a family"; and I would add "divorced," to this list as well. He asked us to "seek excellence in all [our] righteous endeavors, and in all aspects of [our] lives." He comforted those who are grieving over the loss of a husband, those who have not yet experienced marriage, those whose options are being slowly restricted by age or illness—and by implication he asked us to reach out to each other as we experience these moments. He asked us to be wise in setting our priorities so that we will not neglect our "eternal assignments," including motherhood. He asked us to "pursue and . . . achieve . . . education," to "sharpen the skills you have been given." He reminded, "You need, more and more, to feel the perfect love which our Father in Heaven has for you and to sense the value he places upon you as an individual."[2]

Isn't that glorious! As I read through this list, I hope some questions came to your mind, questions like: What skills could I sharpen? Do I need to adjust my priorities? Is there someone whose burden I could lift?

But there are a few questions I'm sure at least some of us are asking ourselves: "Why haven't I done all of these simple things already? I'm sure all of my neighbors are doing them. How can I ever be the kind of woman President Kimball is talking about? What's wrong with me?" Feeling guilty and blaming ourselves certainly does launch us on a process, but I don't think it's a process we enjoy very much! I think we need to lighten up and give ourselves credit for trying.

Now, let's talk in a little more detail about three of the ideas that President Kimball touched on: the strength of our diversity, the power of personal spirituality, and how we can enjoy both processes more through asking better, more thoughtful questions about them.

Let's start by talking about the strength that comes through diversity. Remember when President Kimball said that he wanted women of the Church to be "distinct and different—in happy ways"? I don't think he was just talking about being different from women of the world. A lot of women of the world are like us. That's why they'll join us. That's why all of the women who have joined the Church since April 1979 are among us today. We need to be a living, thriving, caring sisterhood that respects individuals, fosters their gifts, and lets them serve each other. So let's ask some questions about our sisterhood. I just want you to think about them silently.

— How many women in Relief Society would you say are your close friends?
— If you needed help, whom would you call?
— Is there at least one other person in Relief Society for whom you feel responsible because you love her?
— Do you enjoy going to Relief Society? Do you like what you hear there?
— Do you feel that your opinions are heard and respected?
— At Relief Society, do you feel cherished for your uniqueness or valued for your sameness?

There aren't any right or wrong answers to these questions. Maybe you've already been asking some of them. Maybe asking them was a new experience for you. I hope that for all of you Relief Society is a nourishing, enriching place to be. But I know that for a lot of women it's not. We encounter too many faithful women, who have strong testimonies and who serve devotedly, but who feel that they have to fit into a "mold" to really be accepted at Relief Society. Non-traditional women—working women, divorced women, and single mothers—particularly feel this way. Don't you think a good question would be why they do? If you're one of these women who have these feelings of

not-quite-belonging, is there some way you can share these feelings with the Relief Society president? Or with another sister?
Or, ideally, with the whole group? I hope so. And if you're a sister who feels pretty much in the mainstream, is there something
you could do to show a woman who may feel "different" that
you value her diversity and cherish her individuality? I have a
lot of confidence in the ability of Mormon sisters to ask excellent questions like these.

The next step in the important process of getting an answer
is to take your questions thoughtfully to the Lord in honesty
and faith, with the assurance that he loves you and wants to
help you find answers.

Sometimes Relief Society sisters are worried if they aren't
the same as everyone else. Sometimes they get concerned if
some sisters seem to have different thoughts, opinions, or feelings than they do. How should we feel about diversity? How
should we deal with differences? Surely with love and respect!
How else can we truly follow Christ? Are differences bad? In my
opinion, differences are great!

Elder John Carmack wrote a wonderful *Ensign* article urging:
"Each of us should be fair to everyone, especially the victims of
discrimination, isolation, and exclusion. Let us be careful not to
snicker at jokes that demean and belittle others because of religious, cultural, racial, national, or gender differences. All are
alike unto God. We should walk away or face up to the problem
when confronted with these common and unworthy practices."
This timely reminder called on us to find unity in our shared
faith in Christ and in the Church's customary practices. He
specifically counseled us not to fall into the trap of labeling and
stereotyping each other: "Labeling a fellow Church member an
intellectual, a less-active member, a feminist, a South African,
an Armenian, a Utah Mormon, or a Mexican, for example,
seemingly provides an excuse to mistreat or ignore that
person."[3]

How often do we ask in Relief Society, in church, or in
community groups, "Is this fair? Do I like being treated this
way? I wonder how Susan or Maria or Gretta feels about this?"

Maybe we should ask these questions a little more often. When we ask better questions, the Lord can give us better answers. When we remember President Kimball's statement that Mormon women should be "distinct and different—in happy ways," then we start to get the vision of diversity's power to help us grow together.

And now let's talk about the second concept, the power of personal spirituality. There are so many elements of spirituality that it's hard to single out just one, but let's focus for a few minutes on praying with real questions in mind, being honest and real in our prayers. I want to tell you a story of a miracle, as told by a woman missionary in Papua, New Guinea, who was involved in Christian service particularly to the women. These women worshipped ancestor spirits—they weren't even Christian—but they needed a miracle. Even if we're not farmers, we know what it's like when the weather isn't cooperating. In the village of Managalasi, where Jaki was working with the people, she worried along with the people as eight weeks passed—two months of the rainy season—but with no rain. "The ground in the gardens hardened like cement. Carefully planted yams shriveled under the punishing sun." Clouds came, but they never yielded rain. The rituals of the shamans did no good. The prayers to ancestor spirits produced no results. The teenage boys placed certain stones and vines, that were supposed to have a magical effect, around the gardens, "but nothing worked." The water spring slowly dried up. "The entire land cried out for water; and with each day, anxiety climbed with the thermometer."

Under a beautiful, starlit sky, Jaki walked to the women's Bible study class where the women had gathered. They greeted her warmly. The hostess's smile was broad and warm, revealing "two rows of blood-red teeth stained from chewing betel nut," but her whole attitude was of cordial hospitality as she spread a mat for Jaki. Jaki shook hands with all of the women, looking into each face.

They were tired, worn-out faces. Perspiration had formed roadways on their soot-smeared foreheads and cheeks.

"How are you?" I asked each lady in turn.

"No rain," they answered, as though that were the standard answer.

Then one of the women, called out from a back wall, asking Jaki to pray for rain. Urgently the woman said, "If it doesn't rain tonight, our gardens will be completely destroyed. We'll all starve." The other women joined in the desperate chorus. They knew what would happen—sick babies, weakened oldsters, starvation, and thirst.

Listening to them, Jaki realized they were right. Some of them would die if it did not rain, but she felt panicky. The sky was absolutely cloudless, spangled with stars. She knew there was no chance of rain. Yet they were begging her, "Ask God to make it rain *tonight!*" She was stunned by their faith. "These women—women who prayed to ancestor spirits—were now willing to trust a foreigner's God as though He were their only hope." Their eyes clung to hers as she hesitated:

> Frantically, I sent an SOS to God: "Lord, what on earth should I tell these women?" A verse leaped to mind: "Whatsoever ye shall ask, I will do it." I knew God was putting His promise into my thoughts and wanting me to trust Him now.
>
> I felt the panic leave my body and God's peace take control. "OK," I said, clearing my throat. I saw relief spread over their faces, as if I had removed a load of firewood from their heads.

And so, Jaki began to pray. She prayed for each woman by name, praying that her garden would produce abundant food and that no one in her family would go hungry. She prayed her way around the room, peeking, when she needed to, to be sure that she didn't overlook anyone. And she ended her prayer with the fervent plea, "And, Lord, send the rain tonight!"

The women "looked satisfied" as the prayer concluded, and settled down to listen attentively to Jaki's lesson. Twenty minutes later, they heard a faint patter on the roof, and then a pelting.

. . . The rain spattered in through the windows. It dripped through openings in the old weather-faded house. Excitement swept through the room in a wild frenzy. Some of the women hugged each other.

I searched for [Namiji]. She sat, leaning against the wall. Her tears, mixed with soot and perspiration, formed a dark liquid in the deep pockets below her eyes. . . . There was no question in anyone's mind that it was God who had sent the rain. The room blurred as a feeling of happiness shivered up and down my body. I sensed the presence of the Lord with us in the room. No words could express my complete joy to God.[4]

This Christian missionary asked an empowering question. She didn't ask, "How can I make it rain?" She asked, "Lord, what do you want me to tell these women?" Sometimes we think we can do it by ourselves, that it will make us strong to struggle through a problem alone. Or sometimes we think that no one can help us, no one can understand us. The Savior can and will do both. James 1:5 is that wonderful scripture that gave the boy Joseph Smith courage to go out into the Sacred Grove. Let's paraphrase it so that it applies to us more directly: "When we lack wisdom, we should ask God. God will give us wisdom generously, without scolding and finding fault. Wisdom *will be given* to us." I think that God is waiting for us to ask him. He wants to give to us and give generously, and he will not scold or reproach us. He doesn't say, "Can't you figure this out on your own?" or "You, again! Didn't I just see you this morning?" No, he's anxious to fill our souls with his goodness and his love. Our questions are just as important to us as Joseph Smith's question was to him. And who knows, maybe the Lord has an answer for us that turns out to be as important to the world as Joseph Smith's answer was to us today!

It is so important that we come unto Christ, that we minister to others, that we truly lay hold on the promise and motto of Relief Society, "Charity never faileth."

However, it is possible that all our good works may become just a list of chores and duties until we let the Spirit of Jesus Christ fill our hearts. The prophet Nephi reminds us that we should seek the Spirit whenever we serve. "But behold, I say unto you that ye must pray always, and not faint; that ye must not perform any thing unto the Lord save in the first place ye shall pray unto the Father in the name of Christ, that he will consecrate thy performance unto thee, that thy performance may be for the welfare of thy soul" (2 Nephi 32:9).

Eliza R. Snow said, "It is the duty of each one of us to be a holy woman. We shall have elevated aims, if we are holy women. We shall feel that we are called to perform important duties. No one is exempt from them. There is no sister so isolated, and her sphere so narrow but what she can do a great deal towards establishing the Kingdom of God upon the earth."[5] Do we see ourselves as holy women? Do we feel the stirring within ourselves that draws us toward holiness? Do we realize that each choice we make for good, each kindness, each act of cherishing another's freedom and diversity, each honoring of our own agency all help establish righteousness on the earth?

Well, have I convinced you that something special will happen if you start to ask better questions? I hope I have. I hope, too, that you'll be patient while you're struggling for answers. Not all questions have answers. And even when answers come, they can't always be implemented quickly. But unless we start with the questions, there will never be any hope of changing and growing and making new room for revelation to work. I'm excited about the questions that you will ask in the weeks and months to come. I hope that they have to do with personal spirituality and with diversity. And when things get perhaps too solemn and intense, I hope someone will ask, "Wasn't there something about lightening up?" And I hope that you'll develop many, many questions of your own.

The Doctrine and Covenants talks about Church officers being "upheld by the confidence, faith, and prayer of the church" (D&C 107:22). I have felt upheld in that way, and I want you to know that I uphold you. I uphold you with all the confidence and faith of my heart. I uphold you with prayer, daily and nightly. Elaine Jack, Aileen Clyde, and I pray for you, alone and as a presidency. We pray that the power of your callings will rest upon you and that the might of your sisterhood may break the shackles of tradition and limitation and unleash a great flood of righteousness upon the earth in these latter days, that we may act in the power of the Savior as holy women in his kingdom.

Notes

1. Spencer W. Kimball, "Let Us Move Forward and Upward," *Ensign*, May 1979, p. 82.

2. Spencer W. Kimball, "The Role of Righteous Women," *Ensign*, November 1979, pp. 102–4.

3. John K. Carmack, "Unity in Diversity," *Ensign*, March 1991, p. 9.

4. Jaki Parlier, "First of the Miracles," *Signs of the Times*, August 1991, pp. 30–31.

5. Eliza R. Snow, as quoted under date of 20 June, in *1992 Engagement Calendar: Commemorating 150 Years of Relief Society*, created by Jana Erickson (Salt Lake City: Bookcraft, 1991).

6

Change and Our Choices

*W*hen I was a young woman, being Japanese was not a
very popular thing to be. I saw that situation slowly
change, until Japan was honored for the unmatched quality of
its superb technical achievement. And now we're at a time
where Japan and America aren't getting along too well again.
There's always change, isn't there? I want to talk about three
different aspects of change: first, things that we can't change;
second, change that we don't choose but where we have some
control over how we respond to change; and third, change that
we can initiate, choose, and control.

Things We Can't Change

When we talk about things we can't change, it always reminds me of one of my favorite Calvin and Hobbes cartoons. I
wouldn't say that Calvin is a typical first-grader, but he certainly

This address was originally given to the Lambda Delta Sigma unit at the University of Utah,
1 March 1992.

has the spunk and energy of one. And everybody needs a friend with the wisdom of his stuffed tiger, Hobbes. Hobbes observes: "A new decade is coming up."

Calvin complains, "Yeah, Big Deal! Humph! Where are the flying cars? Where are the moon colonies? Where are the personal robots and the zero gravity boots, huh? You call this a new decade? You call this the future? Ha! Where are the rocket packs? Where are the disintegration rays? Where are the floating cities?"

Hobbes interjects, "Frankly, I'm not sure people have the brains to manage the technology they've *got*."

Calvin continues, unchecked, "I mean *look* at this! We still have *weather*!! Give me a break!"[1]

Well, we do have weather. We haven't been able to change that yet. And I think it's probably just fine that we can't. Weather makes me happy. But there are other things we can't change that we wish we could. We call these other things "adversity," and none of us likes it very much. Carlfred Broderick, who is head of the marriage and family therapist program at the University of Southern California and a former bishop and stake president—not to mention the father of eight children— described this situation as realistically as I've ever heard it. He was attending a program for eleven-year-old Primary girls who would enter the Young Women's program that year. The officers had really knocked themselves out to create the Land of Oz right there in the cultural hall, together with a yellow brick road and the four companions—Dorothy, the tin woodsman, the cowardly lion, and the scarecrow. They were all singing songs about the gospel. The city of Oz, a mural on one side of the cultural hall, looked a lot like the Los Angeles Temple. (President Broderick's stake was in California.) As they danced down the yellow brick road, President Broderick noticed something: "There were no weeds on that road; there were no munchkins; there were no misplaced tiles; there was no wicked witch of the west. That was one antiseptic yellow brick road, and it was very, very clear that once they got to Oz, they had it made. It was all sewed up."

This bothered President Broderick a little, and he was

bothered a little more when the next event on the program was a beautiful sister "who I swear was sent over from Hollywood central casting" with a perfectly handsome returned-missionary husband, also from central casting, and several pretty children straight out of "Kleenex ads" who provided moral support while she "enthused over her temple marriage and how wonderful life was with her charming husband and her perfect children and that the young women too could look like her and have a husband like him and children like them if they would stick to the yellow brick road and live in Oz."

So after President Broderick had listened to this, the stake Primary president asked him if he wanted to add anything and he promptly said yes. And this is what he told those eleven-year-old girls:

> Girls, this has been a beautiful program. I commend the gospel with all of its auxiliaries and the temple to you, but I do not want you to believe for one minute that if you keep all the commandments and live as close to the Lord as you can and do everything right and fight off the entire priests quorum one by one and wait chastely for your missionary to return and pay your tithing and attend your meetings, accept calls from the bishop, and have a temple marriage, I do not want you to believe that bad things will not happen to you. And when that happens, I do not want you to say that God was not true. Or, to say, "They promised me in Primary, they promised me when I was a Mia Maid, they promised me from the pulpit that if I were very, very good, I would be blessed. But the boy I want doesn't know I exist, or the missionary I've waited and kept chaste [for] so we both could go to the temple turned out to be a flake," or far worse things than any of the above. Sad things—children who are sick or developmentally handicapped, husbands who are not faithful, illnesses that can cripple, or violence, betrayals, hurts, deaths, losses—when those things happen, do not say, God is not keeping His promises to me.
>
> The gospel of Jesus Christ is not insurance against pain. It is resource in event of pain, and when that pain comes (and it will come because we came here on earth to have pain among other things), when it comes, rejoice that you have resource to deal with your pain.[2]

Well, that was President Broderick's message. No matter how good you are, bad things can happen to you. I think that was a great message for eleven-year-old girls to hear. I don't know if eleven-year-old girls understood it. I'm sure some of them did. If the national statistics hold true, perhaps one in three of those girls in that audience, LDS or not LDS, had been or would be sexually abused before they turned eighteen. Perhaps another one in ten were growing up in a home with only one parent. Some of them would not find that returned missionary. If they went to the temple, they would go on their own. Some of those girls would be dead before they were eighteen—dead from disease, from accidents, and from the random violence that devastates our society. It's a good message for women of any age to hear. Eighteen-year-old women are members of the Relief Society. The Church thinks of them as women—maybe not as wise as their grandmothers yet, but certainly with that capability, maybe not as hardworking and loving as their mothers yet, but definitely with that potential; sisters of the Savior, and certainly with the capability of becoming holy women.

So I want you to remember President Broderick's comment: "The gospel is not insurance against pain." It is reassurance when pain comes. Ezekiel says: "And they shall comfort you, when ye see their ways and their doings: and ye shall know that I have not done without cause all that I have done in it, saith the Lord God" (Ezekiel 14:23); and the Apostle Paul says consolingly:

> For whatsoever things were written aforetime were written for our learning, that we through patience and comfort of the scriptures might have hope.
> Now the God of patience and consolation grant you to be likeminded one toward another according to Christ Jesus:
> That ye may with one mind and one mouth glorify God, even the Father of our Lord Jesus Christ.
> Wherefore receive ye one another, as Christ also received us to the glory of God. (Romans 15:4–7.)

This, in my opinion, is the comfort of the gospel: when evil enters our lives, we can still be assured that Christ is with us, even in the depths of our suffering.

Choosing Our Response to Change

So, change is inevitable. Sometimes it's awful. Sometimes it's great. But often, we have no control over change. What we can choose, in many, many circumstances, is our response to change. I saw a bumper sticker the other day. It was on the back of a pickup that had quite a lot of reading material on it. One bumper sticker advised people to have a happy day, another advertised the owner's favorite country and western station, and a third suggested that people who didn't like his driving should "stay off the sidewalk." But it also had a bumper sticker that said: "Hard-hat Construction Area: Christian under Construction."

I loved that bumper sticker. That's what we are, isn't it? We're all Christians under construction, and that's an area where we need hard hats. It's hard work, even a little risky sometimes, and it's no place for softies who lack discipline.

I taught elementary school for years and I love the honesty of children, so one of the books I really prize is a collection called *Children's Letters to God*. In this book, kids ask God questions, real questions, questions they're confused about or have wondered about for a long time but haven't found a grownup who can answer them. One of my favorite questions comes from a little boy named Tommy. He wrote: "Dear God, I want to be just like you when I am your age. OK?"[3] I think Tommy knows a lot about the hard-hat zone in which the construction of Christians takes place. The gospel is change. Repentance is change.

I remember watching a PBS program on motion. It showed how a herd of wildebeest running away from a lion all pivots and dashes together. If they didn't move—if they didn't change their location—they would be dead. The program also showed that it is the motion of the electrons that keeps the atom stable. If those electrons should stop moving, the atom would disintegrate. Living processes are possible because of types of movement like dialysis, osmosis, and diffusion.

Change is happening to all of us. All of us grow older. We're seventeen, then eighteen, and then suddenly you're as old as I am. We have no control over this kind of change. It happens to all of us. But we make some choices associated with those changes. All college women chose to make the transition from high school to college instead of to some other setting. I hope that all eighteen-year-old LDS women also choose to make the transition from Young Women into Relief Society. We need them there. And they need Relief Society. Our physical lives will cease to exist without the constant renewal of eating and digestion, without exercise and rest. Our spiritual lives will also come to a halt and disintegrate without the constant renewal of scripture study, personal prayer, and church attendance. Change will continue to happen.

We can't always choose what happens to us, but we can choose how we respond. Sometimes change scares us or hurts us. Sometimes we feel resentful about change or inadequate to it. That's when it helps to remember my favorite Japanese proverb from the ancient book of Okazaki chapter one, verse one: Lighten up! We can always respond better, even to difficult things, if we can retain even a little lightheartedness.

Change We Can Choose

The third kind of change is change we choose. Alma tells us: "Choose ye this day, whom ye will serve." Then he continues, "Now if a man [or woman] . . . believed in God it was his privilege to serve him." (Alma 30:8–9.) So this is a wonderful choice that the gospel offers us. Not everybody makes a good choice when presented with this decision. One friend of mine had a daughter who went to a church college but chose to go sit in the bars. She didn't finish school, she got pregnant and had to get married, she devastated her parents' life, she short-circuited her education, she abused her body, and she brought a child into the world under conditions that weren't fair to that baby. She made some bad choices—but she still has the capability of making good choices, choices that will turn her life in a new direction, choices that will increase her options and those of her husband and children.

I want to talk with you very seriously today about expanding your choices. Janet G. Lee, the wife of the president of Brigham Young University, told a very poignant story about her daughter. She said:

> When my daughter Stephanie was five years old I took her to register for kindergarten. When we arrived, she was invited to go into a classroom to "play games" with the teachers and other children. As a former elementary school teacher, I was certain that the "games" were a method of testing for placement purposes.
>
> A teacher was sitting just outside the room with a box of crayons and several sheets of blank paper; and I smiled confidently to myself from across the hall as Stephanie was asked to choose her favorite color and write her name. "She could write *all* the names in our family," I thought to myself. "She is so well prepared, there isn't anything in that room she can't handle." But Stephanie just stood there. The teacher repeated the instructions, and again my daughter stood still, staring blankly at the box of crayons, with her knees locked and her hands behind her back.
>
> In the sweet, patient voice that teachers use when they are beginning to feel slightly *im*patient, the teacher asked once more, "Stephanie, choose your favorite color, dear, and write your name on this paper." I was about to come to my daughter's aid when the teacher kindly said, "That's okay. We will help you learn to write your name when you come to school in the fall." With all the restraint I could gather, I watched Stephanie move into the classroom with a teacher who believed my daughter did not know how to write her name.
>
> On the way home, I tried to ask as nonchalantly as possible why she had not written her name. "I couldn't," she replied. "The teacher said to choose my favorite color, and there wasn't a pink crayon in the box!"

Sister Lee commented:

> How many times are we, as Heavenly Father's children, immobilized because the choice we had in mind for ourselves just isn't available to us, at least not at the time we want it?

Is progress halted when acceptance into a chosen major is denied, when enrollment in a required class is closed, when a desired job doesn't come through, when that dream date doesn't progress beyond friendship, or when the money hoped for isn't there? Are we ever, for reasons that are hard to understand or beyond our control, faced with a set of circumstances that we did not have in mind for ourselves? In other words, what happens when we look in the box, and the pink crayon just isn't there?[4]

Sister Lee's point is a good one. It's the same point, basically, as President Broderick's. But I also see another lesson in it for us as Latter-day Saints who understand our power of choice. Stephanie at age five may not have understood that she had some options. One of those options was to say, "My favorite crayon is pink. Will you please find me a pink crayon?" Another option was to say, "I don't see my favorite crayon there, but I see my next-favorite crayon. May I use that?" In other words, Stephanie could have asked some questions about the experience that was being presented to her.

Sometimes we tend not to ask questions about options because we feel that we need to think, believe, and act the same way as everyone else. There are different ways we can react. We can choose to be passive or active, to ask questions or be silent, conform to social pressure or resist the status quo. I think women need to make more active choices more of the time.

I think that sometimes even at church, where the wonderful diversity of the gospel is available to us all, women sometimes get messages that inadvertently reinforce passivity. Many women feel that there is a Relief Society "mold" that they have to fit into to be acceptable. I love the experience of Karen Lynn Davidson, a stake Relief Society president in California. She said that "the people who were the most surprised" when she was called to that position were the ones who knew her best. Why? Because she was nothing like the traditional Relief Society president:

At mealtime, when people in my house ask, "Is this home-made?" they're hoping the answer is no. . . . I teach at a Catholic girls' school; I was single until I was thirty-eight years old; I have no children of my own—I'm that other kind of mother that usually has the adjective *wicked* in front of it—a stepmother.

Then she says—and I love this!

> But paradoxically, I serve an important purpose by not fitting the traditional image. It would be difficult for someone in my stake to look me in the eye and say, "I just don't think I fit the Relief Society mold!" I'm a daily reminder to our stake . . . that the umbrella of The Church of Jesus Christ of Latter-day Saints is large and welcoming. It is not made to shelter one kind of woman only. . . . There's room for all of us, and what happiness we can find as we use our individual powers to teach, bless, and strengthen one another![5]

The Apostle Paul tells us, "where the Spirit of the Lord is, there is liberty" (2 Corinthians 3:17). How do you think he would feel about women leaving meetings of the Lord's church feeling confined? The Apostle James said, "If any of you lack wisdom, let [her] ask of God, that giveth to all . . . liberally, and upbraideth not; and it shall be given [her]" (James 1:5). How do you suppose he would feel about women thinking that they mustn't ask questions because that would make them unacceptable to their sisters in the meeting?

I hope that every sister who attends Relief Society, every Relief Society officer, and every Relief Society teacher will think compassionately and seriously about how to bring more flexibility, more responsiveness to needs, and more respect for diversity into her own Relief Society. That's a positive change that would benefit individuals, LDS women in general, and the institution.

Let me tell you a personal story about an experience I had with change. I had the opportunity to choose it, to take an active role in promoting it, and to help it be a positive change. When I was a principal in Colorado, my district built a new elementary school—a four-track year-round school. When the district first proposed this type of school, the goal was to take care of both the needs of the district for a new elementary school and also to house some of the different programs. This was a wonderful opportunity. My superintendent, with the school board's approval, asked me to head up the new school. I was thrilled and excited.

However, year-round school was a change, a departure from the norm; and some parents reacted with alarm. They opposed the change and came to the Board of Education meetings to protest. As the newly appointed principal, I had six months while the school was being constructed to solve this problem. I knew that if the parents didn't want their children there and that if they were compelled to come, all of us were going to have a bad experience. I believed in this school. I knew that what it could do was something wonderful for the students and the community. So I took on the job of community relations.

I persuaded the Board of Education to take a big risk. I said: "I think it's really important that we avoid compulsion with a closed enrollment policy. I think we must assure parents that they can still choose the school with the traditional schedule if that's what they truly wish. But I promise you that our elementary school will have three-quarters of the students it's supposed to have when it opens—that the parents will change their minds, will support this new school, and will help us make it work." So they agreed to let me try.

So, I had a school to finish, a faculty to hire, a curriculum to plan, and a four-track schedule to work out. And now I had to sell the idea to the parents of over six hundred children. How on earth could I do that?

I thought about important principles of the gospel that could help. I had already come down squarely for the most important principle: choice. By insisting that the parents be able to choose either school, I honored their agency. The second most important principle of the gospel, in my opinion, is progress—line upon line, precept upon precept. And that means communication, continuous ongoing communication. I needed to communicate with the parents. They needed to know that I understood them, that I respected them, and that I considered them partners in learning.

And the third important principle was love. I wanted those parents to know that I loved their children already, I loved learning, and I loved to see children learning. I knew that that was what parents really wanted for their children, too.

These three principles made it easy to see how to achieve my task. I had to spend time with the parents in small groups so that we could all talk, all listen. They needed to know me and the teachers. I needed to know them and their children. This couldn't happen in just one encounter, either. So that was the commitment: small groups, ongoing discussions, and a long period of time.

I had worked closely with the PTA of the school that covered the area to be served by Sunrise Elementary, so I contacted a few key women and included them as part of my strategic planning team. We sat down with a map and divided up the area so that we pinpointed a key couple every few blocks. Then we asked this couple to invite the parents of five or six families in the immediate neighborhood to a meeting with us. These meetings were held in homes. I would go with two or three of my teachers. First we would listen, then we would talk. We would explain what Sunrise Elementary planned to do and hoped to do, how it would work for the children, and how the parents could help. We listened to their complaints, their questions, their protests. We answered their questions, we tried to see things from their point of view, and we tried to include them.

After only a few weeks of these meetings, I could tell that the mood was changing. The parents didn't know the system, and they didn't trust it; but they started to trust us as they knew us. For six months, every week, I went to at least one of these meetings. If a family couldn't come on the night of the first invitation, we made sure they were invited to a later meeting.

Meanwhile, the school was being built. I was interviewing and hiring teachers. My office was a trailer parked on the construction site. Every day, I would put on my hard hat and walk over the building as it slowly grew. I worked with the curriculum specialists planning the quadruple track and the schedule.

The year ended. Time came for student registration. As the parents came in to register their children, I was at the office to greet them. Or as they mailed in their registration forms, I looked at the names. I knew eighty-five percent of those parents personally, and I knew one hundred percent of the names. Only three families had chosen to keep their children at the old school; and all three of those families transferred their children before Christmas.

What if I had said, "Oh, no! This is a change! I'm scared! Oh, no! Some parents are opposed to this idea! I don't want any conflict! What if I can't change their minds!" In other words, what if I had let fear do the talking when the wonderful opportunity that this change represented came along? I would have missed some of the best years of my professional life.

Conclusion

I have confidence in the women of this Church. They can be change-bringers. They aren't stuck merely with enduring graciously what happens to them—although there will be some of that. Nor are they limited simply to having a good attitude as change that they did not choose impacts them. They can make change happen. They can be bridge-builders between the old and the new. They can see visions. They can dream dreams. They can make new realities. This promise of the Lord is to them:

> And it shall come to pass . . . that I will pour out my spirit upon all flesh; and your sons and your daughters shall prophesy, your old men shall dream dreams, your young men shall see visions:
>
> And also upon the servants and upon the handmaids in those days will I pour out my spirit.
>
> And I will shew wonders in the heavens and in the earth. . . .
>
> And . . . whosoever shall call on the name of the Lord shall be delivered. (Joel 2:28–32.)

The prophet Ezekiel also had a strange and powerful vision that I think applies to our days. It is a vision of how the Spirit of the Lord and the spirit of the gospel can heal that which is broken, purify that which is polluted, and become a source of spiritual strength and joy if we choose to live gospel principles. In this vision, Ezekiel stood before the door of the temple and he saw water springing up from under the altar and flowing away to the east. And the messenger who was with Ezekiel took him along the edge of that stream of water, following where the waters went. Every so often, he would stop and measure the water; and each time he did it was deeper. First, it was just to his ankles. A thousand paces further on, it had reached his knees. Then it was up to his thighs. And then it was so deep that a person could not pass over it. The waters were running through a desert, but as Ezekiel watched, trees sprang up at the edge of the water—beautiful, healthy trees, trees that bore fruit, trees that bore new fruit according to their months. Next the waters poured into the sea and healed the waters of the sea. An abundance of fish came into being in the waters, swarming and swimming through the water so that fishers could stand on either bank and draw out food for their people. The messenger summarized, "And every thing shall live whither the river cometh. . . . because their waters . . . issued out of the sanctuary." (Ezekiel 47:1–12.)

You may feel like a sandy and barren desert. You may feel like a bitter salt marsh. The changes that have come to you may have wounded you and hurt you. You may feel that an ocean flood has washed away all of your moorings and you are drowning without anything to cling to. Go to the sanctuary. Drink the healing waters. Cling to the gospel. "I am the Lord," says Jesus Christ. "I change not." (Malachi 3:6.) That is a promise we can rely on as change surrounds us. There are more changes that must and will come. Some of those changes you will not be able to do anything about. Others you will be able to influence. And still others you will be able to cause.

One of my favorite hymns is "Abide with Me!" The second verse reads in part:

Change and decay in all around I see;
O thou who changest not, abide with me!

The Savior is with you. And he wants you to know that he is with you. At your loneliest moments, he stands at the door and knocks. Let this be a time when you really learn the power of prayer, when you become so sensitive to the whisperings of the Holy Ghost that you can greet new experiences with love and purity, when the scriptures become the bread of life and the water of joy to you. Empowerment comes when we realize his matchless love, the power of his atoning sacrifice to transform our lives, and the absolute steadfastness of his presence in our lives.

Notes

1. Bill Watterson, *Scientific Progress Goes "Boink": A Calvin and Hobbes Collection* (Kansas City, MO: Andrews and McMeel Books, 1991), p. 31.

2. Carlfred Broderick, "The Uses of Adversity," in *As Women of Faith: Talks Selected from the BYU Women's Conferences,* edited by Mary E. Stovall and Carol Cornwall Madsen (Salt Lake City: Deseret Book Company, 1989), pp. 171–73.

3. Eric Marshall and Stuart Hample, comps., *Children's Letters to God,* enl. ed. (New York: Pocket Books, 1975), not paginated.

4. Janet G. Lee, "Winter Devotional" (not titled), 14 January 1992, p. 1. Photocopy of typescript in my possession.

5. Karen Lynn Davidson, in *Women and the Power Within: To See Life Steadily and See It Whole,* edited by Dawn Hall Anderson and Marie Cornwall (Salt Lake City: Deseret Book Company, 1991), pp. 7–8.

7

Five Tips on Making Better Mistakes

I hope we all have a keen interest in mistakes. Just in case you think you don't have any particular interest in mistakes, let me give you a little quiz. You won't need paper and pencil. You can answer it in your head. It's true-false, to make it even easier. Here it is:

All human beings make mistakes. True or false?

Well, if you answered "true," then there are probably some thoughts on this topic that we can share. I have five tips to help us all make better mistakes.

Principle One: Be Willing to Make Mistakes

We all need to be willing to make mistakes. You know, I was a teacher for twenty-three years and a principal for another ten,

This address was originally presented as a workshop for BYU—Hawaii women's conference, 13–24 April 1992, with additional material from the BYU—Hawaii women's conference on 23 April 1992, a sacrament meeting in a singles ward in Erie Stake, 12 May 1991; and the graduation address at Mountain View High School, Orem, Utah, 26 May 1992.

and I've been a human being for sixty-six years. I know that one of the most important things a teacher can do in creating an environment for learning is to give children permission to make mistakes. (If you stop and think about it, according to this criterion, God is an outstanding teacher—A+!)

I like the proverb: "He [or she] who makes no mistakes does not usually make anything." I would rather make a mistake while I'm making *something* than do nothing for fear of making a mistake. Whenever I am faced with a challenge where I have a high probability of making a mistake and the failure will have conspicuous consequences, I think of cheese soufflés. Let me explain why.

I was fourteen when World War II began. My parents were Japanese plantation laborers. They weren't interned, but severe gas rationing was immediately imposed. Our little village was eleven or twelve miles away from the town of Honomakau, where the middle school was, and gas was available only for the elementary school buses. We faced a dilemma. Should I stop going to high school and hope that the war would end soon? Should I move to the town and keep going to school? If I did that, what would we do for money? My parents and I talked it over. Somehow, there was only one real choice: I must get my education. I think this was an extraordinary decision, especially for a Japanese family and especially for the only daughter of that family with three sons.

So I moved to the town and became a maid for a couple who taught orchestra and English at school. It was very hard. At the age of fourteen, I was in charge of the food budget. I would get up at five o'clock, cook breakfast, clean house, make the beds, and go off to school at eight-thirty. When I came home in the afternoon, I would shop, clean, and cook dinner, then study in the evening until eleven or twelve o'clock. I had learned to cook Japanese food in my own home, of course; and I had helped the cook in the fine American house of Captain Beck, who was in charge of the plantation, so I knew a little about American cooking.

But then one day Mrs. Ehrlich told me that they would be giving a dinner party on Friday evening and asked me to make a cheese soufflé. She showed me where the recipe was and said, "You might want to try it once before Friday." Fortunately, there was also a photograph in the cookbook, because I couldn't imagine how on earth I could make eggs cook so they made a fluffy cake. I stared and stared at that photograph. I read and reread the recipe, visualizing every step. And then I took a deep breath. It was obvious to me that success depended on cooking it very quickly and evenly at a very high temperature for a short period of time. And I wasn't sure how on earth I could possibly do that.

You see, kitchens in Hawaii during World War II were not exactly the glamour locales you see in *Better Homes and Gardens* these days. The stove was a little kerosene range with no built-in oven. In fact, when I wanted to bake something, I would take a tin box that was open on the bottom and put it on top of one of the kerosene burners. It had reflecting sides and a rack in the middle, and the heat would all come from the open flame at the bottom. Naturally, since the bottom was open, a lot of the heat escaped. Since there was no thermometer, you had to adjust it by turning the flame up or down, guessing whether you were making it too hot or not hot enough. And since there wasn't a window into the box, there was no way to see what was happening inside that box without pulling down its rickety little door and letting a lot of the heat escape.

So you can see why I took a deep breath. Eggs, fortunately, weren't one of the things that had become rare during wartime. Cheese was more difficult to come by since it had to be imported, but I knew I needed that practice. I laid out the eggs, the mixing bowl, the wooden spoon (there was no such thing as a mixer during World War II, either) and the salt and pepper. I turned on the kerosene and put the tin box on the top. Then I prayed. I prayed very sincerely to Heavenly Father to help me follow the recipe exactly, to help me know when each step of the recipe was being done correctly, and how to regulate the temperature so that the soufflé would cook all the way through without either burning or falling. Then I beat up those eggs by hand, until they were fluffy and light, and I stirred in a prayer with every beat of the spoon.

My mother had taught me how to tell the temperature inside the oven by putting my hand in it. You could hold your hand in a medium-hot oven for about two or three seconds without much discomfort. If you couldn't, then the oven was very hot. If you could hold your hand in there longer, then the oven was too cold.

So I popped it into the oven. Then I pulled up a hard, straight-backed kitchen chair and sat right in front of the oven. I kept my eyes fixed on that oven as though the gas would go out if I blinked. I kept praying. I watched the clock. The recipe book said thirty-five minutes, and I counted every second. I could smell it cooking, but I couldn't tell whether that was bad or good, since I didn't know what it was supposed to smell like. At twenty-five minutes, I eased that little door open just a crack and peeked in as carefully as I could. Sure enough, it was high and fluffy, a bright golden brown.

I quickly eased the door shut again and sat down. I counted those last ten minutes as they went by, a second at a time. I kept sniffing, to see if I could detect the slightest trace of a burned smell. And I kept on praying. At exactly thirty-five minutes, I cautiously eased the oven door open just a crack and peered in again. It was brown. It looked tender and delicious. I started to open the oven door wider, but I had a feeling that it needed just a little longer. I closed the oven door again, sat down, and kept praying.

About three minutes later, I suddenly felt that that time was right. Once more I peered in. Now a strip of darker brown crust had formed around the edge of the mold. The top looked glossy and golden. I shut the kerosene off, whisked the soufflé out of the oven, and took it away to show Mrs. Ehrlich. She clapped her hands in delight. "That's exactly right!" she exclaimed. "Exactly what it's supposed to look like. How wonderful!"

We had it for supper that night. They praised the taste, the texture, the flavor. I nibbled away cautiously, filing the unfamiliar combination of eggs and cheese away in the back of my mind. And that night, I spent a long time on my knees, thanking a Heavenly Father who knew how long it took to cook a soufflé in a kerosene oven.

Well, the end of the story is that the second soufflé was a great hit at the party, and the Ehrlichs often had me make it for them when they entertained. It always turned out, but I don't think I've ever made it since. After all, I think *sukiyaki* tastes better and it's certainly a lot easier to cook! At least for me!

So you can see why I say that whenever something seems very risky or chancy, hard to do, even overwhelming, and when there really aren't any guarantees that I won't make a terrible mistake, I think, "Remember the soufflé, Chieko! You can do this, too!"

Principle Two: Mistakes Are Human, Not Evil

Making a mistake does not mean that we are wicked or stupid. It just means we're human. When we're trying to do our best and we make a mistake, it is not the same thing as being guilty of a sin. The difference between a mistake and a sin lies in two characteristics: first, you must know that one choice is right and another is wrong; and second, you must have the ability to choose between them. In other words, to sin, we must know the law and willfully break the law. We deliberately choose evil over good when we know what the good is.

Do you know anyone who hasn't sinned? I don't. I don't know one single person who hasn't misused his or her agency and brains. Whoops, we still must be human after all! But what's the answer in that case? Is there an eraser big enough for us? The gospel tells us the answer to that question, and the answer is yes!

I appreciated the insights of Marie K. Hafen in an *Ensign* article about repentance and the Atonement:

> Adam and Eve fell that they might have joy. But they didn't skip merrily out of Eden singing and wishing everyone a nice day. They walked in sorrow into a lonely world, where they earned their bread by the sweat of their brows and learned about joy in the midst of misery and pain. Can you imagine how Eve felt when she learned that her son Cain had taken the life of her son Abel and that God had banished Cain?

How could Mother Eve possibly have found joy in the middle of such affliction? She found it by letting the atonement of Christ heal her pain and sanctify her experience. Indeed, her experience with sin and misery played a crucial role in preparing her for the joy she ultimately found. In Eve's own words, "Were it not for our transgression we never should have had seed, and never should have known good and evil, and the joy of our redemption, and the eternal life which God giveth unto all the obedient" (Moses 5:11).[1]

Even though we understand that the transgression and the Fall were essential to the continued progress of humankind—not sins—it was a choice that brought sin into the world, including Cain's murder. During the sorrowful parts of repentance, we need to understand that the Lord is not punishing us. The Lord is teaching us and loving us. There is a sweetness in the repentance process when we realize that we are not alone.

Principle Three: Don't Be Afraid of the Possibility of Error

Life is designed to make us choose. That means life is designed so that we will make mistakes as well as have successes.

Remember, I said that God was an A+ teacher. In many, many situations, we simply do not know what constitutes good. We have to make choices between two unknowns. Or we have to choose between two good things, hoping that we will benefit from the choice. Or we have to choose between two less than desirable alternatives, and hope we will choose the lesser of two evils. Accepting ambiguity is one of the signs of an adult. We cannot predict the consequences of some choices until after we have made the choice. Sometimes it takes years for us to understand the significance of a choice we made.

Jesus volunteered to be our Savior, to atone for our sins, because he had such confidence in the Father's plan and also in our ability to learn to become like the Father. Now, if Heavenly Father and Jesus Christ knew before the organization of the world that we were going to make mistakes and made provisions for it in the plan of salvation, then don't you think we should lighten up on ourselves?

Let me remind you of another great kitchen proverb: "You can't make an omelette without breaking eggs." To me, that proverb gives us permission to take a chance, to risk a little, to make a mistake. Sometimes we want so badly to do everything just right that our desire for perfection paralyzes us. Well, if we're not moving, we can't get closer to our goal. I don't think that the Lord is hovering over us just waiting to pounce on us if we make a mistake. Instead, I think he's behind us, giving us a gentle nudge and saying, "Take one step. That's good. Now try another."

I think that's what the Lord was saying to the Saints in Kirtland when he said, "Wherefore, be not weary in well-doing, for ye are laying the foundation of a great work. And out of small things proceedeth that which is great." (D&C 64:33.) I think that's what Paul was telling the Saints in Philippi when he said, "I can do all things through Christ [who] strengtheneth me" (Philippians 4:13).

In other words, this is where faith comes in. We all have to do hard things in our lives. I'm sixty-six years old and I still have hard things to do in my life. But I know that the loving Father who listened to the prayer of an anxious Japanese-Hawaiian teenager and who made that tin oven cooperate with the soufflé so long ago is the same loving Father who listens to me today. I know he loves me. I know he loves you. And that strength, that help, is available to all of us today.

Now, I certainly took a chance when I married Ed. He was a nonmember, and I know many members of the Church thought, "Well, there goes Chieko. Marrying out of the Church. Lost forever." It was a risk. But I felt we would have a good Christian life together even if he never joined the Church. Because of the kind of man he was I felt confident that he would accept the gospel; and as it turned out, we had a wonderful life together, better than I could have ever imagined.

Our Heavenly Father floods us with choices that we must

make every day—when to get up, what to eat, what to wear, whether to smile or not, what to think about, what to listen to, how to speak to each other. He wants us to practice and practice and practice choosing.

Life isn't a true or false test. It's multiple choice—literally! And on many of the choices, all of the answers are partially right but none is completely right. The only way we can get that problem wrong on the test is to leave it blank. Of course we should make the best choices we can. Of course we should get the best information we can. Of course we should think carefully through our options. Of course we should ponder prayerfully to learn the desires of our Heavenly Father. Of course we should consult with our families and, if appropriate, with our priesthood leaders, with concerned friends, and with specialists who have expertise we may lack. After all, we shouldn't think that, since mistakes are unavoidable, we should try to make as many as possible!

Principle Four: Keep Mistakes in Perspective

It's important to realize that not all choices have life and death significance. Remember that wonderful scripture from the Doctrine and Covenants: "Wherefore, go ye and preach my gospel, whether to the north or to the south, to the east or to the west, *it mattereth not, for ye cannot go amiss*" (D&C 80:3, italics added). Remember, in some cases any choice is the right choice. It just depends on what we make of it.

What are some things in which we cannot "go amiss"? Doing our best. Living the gospel. Being good Christians. We don't even need a formal Church calling to have a wonderful relationship with the Savior and feel happy and committed in service. Once we've stepped out of the waters of baptism, we bear the name of Christ. We don't have to fill out a form and stand in line for it. Once we've been confirmed a member of the Church, we have the gift of the Holy Ghost. We don't have to drive out to the Distribution Center to pick it up. The bishop doesn't have to call us to be a compassionate Christian. We don't have to sign up to be a thoughtful neighbor. The congregation doesn't have to sustain us before we can be kind and sensitive. We don't have to be set apart to love someone. We don't need anyone's permission to do good. We can just go out and do it on our own. Be *kigatsuku*.

Another way of keeping perspective on our mistakes is to review them after a few years and see if they still look like mistakes. Often we will have learned wonderful lessons that we deeply cherish as a result of a mistake that we felt terrible about. One of my favorite books consists of letters that children have written to God with a serious question that they've struggled with and don't know how to get the answer. And one of the most delightful letters in the collection is from a little boy named Herbie. He wrote: "Dear God, My teacher says the north pole is not really at the top. Did you make any other mistakes?"[2] Well, after a few years, Herbie is going to see the location of the North Pole in a much different way. Time has a way of making clear what's a mistake and what isn't.

The word *mistake* (or *mistakes*) doesn't appear very often in the scriptures—just two or three times. But one of those places is in the Book of Mormon where Amulek has just met Alma and is becoming his missionary companion. He explains to the people who he is and who his ancestors are. Then he says:

> And behold, I am also a man of no small reputation among all those who know me; yea, and behold, I have many kindreds and friends, and I have also acquired much riches by the hand of my industry.
>
> Nevertheless, after all this, I never have known much of the ways of the Lord, and his mysteries and marvelous power. I said I never had known much of these things; but behold, I *mistake*, for I have seen much of his mysteries and his marvelous power; yea, even in the preservation of the lives of this people. (Alma 10:4–5, italics added.)

This is the kind of mistake that's good to recognize, isn't it? The Lord is very much involved in our lives. He works constantly for our good; and if we have eyes to see, we will see his "mysteries and marvelous power."

Principle Five: Be Forgiving of Others' Mistakes

Let other people make mistakes too. Apply all of these principles that we're talking about in our own mistakes to our brothers and sisters around us. Refuse to judge. Refuse to compound someone else's mistake or even sin by making it hard for that person to repent.

Do you remember the episode from the New Testament in which Jesus was eating with his disciples and many "publicans and sinners came and sat down with him and his disciples." The Pharisees were scandalized and asked, "Why is he associating with these people?" Jesus heard them, and he answered: "They that be whole need not a physician, but they that are sick. But go ye and learn what that meaneth, I will have mercy, and not sacrifice: for I am not come to call the righteous, but sinners to repentance." (Matthew 9:10–13.) Shouldn't this also be our attitude?

Our Heavenly Father's attitude toward mistakes is that of looking beyond the mistake to the person. Yes, we know that there will be sons of perdition who will have denied the Holy Ghost or shed innocent blood, placing themselves beyond the atonement of the Savior Jesus Christ. But none of us have done any of these things. The Savior's love and mercy extends to all of us. Heavenly Father isn't angry at us for making mistakes. He doesn't expect us to be perfect, he just expects us to be progressing.

It was very moving to me to read an article in the *Church News* about the fiftieth anniversary commemoration services at Pearl Harbor. Over a hundred missionaries contributed their community service hours to help greet guests and usher at the tours and programs where George Bush addressed the survivors and families at 7:55 A.M., the time of the attack, with a larger service following for the public. Two of those missionaries, serving together as companions, had grandfathers who served on oppo-site sides during that war. Elder Yoshiichiro Yamaura of Fukuoka, Japan, is the grandson of Yoshio Yamaura, for whom he was probably named, who was drafted into the Japanese Army. His companion, David Curtis, of Coalville, Utah, is the grandson of Warren Curtis, who served in the Pacific with the engineer corps. This is an example of how the gospel can bridge the gap between cultures to bring peace and reconciliation.[3]

I love the scripture in which the prophet Isaiah addresses God with all the confidence in the world of his power and his love for us:

> Awake, awake, put on strength, O arm of the Lord; awake, as in the ancient days, in the generations of old. Art thou not it that hath cut Rahab, and wounded the dragon?
>
> Art thou not it which hath dried the sea, the waters of the great deep; that hath made the depths of the sea a way for the ransomed to pass over?
>
> Therefore the redeemed of the Lord shall return, and come with singing unto Zion; and everlasting joy shall be upon their head: they shall obtain gladness and joy; and sorrow and mourn-ing shall flee away.
>
> I, even I, am he that comforteth you: who art thou, that thou shouldest be afraid of a man that shall die, and of the son of man which shall be made as grass;
>
> And forgettest the Lord thy maker, that hath stretched forth the heavens, and laid the foundations of the earth; and hast feared continually every day because of the fury of the oppressor, as if he were ready to destroy? and where is the fury of the oppres-sor? . . .
>
> But I am the Lord thy God, that divided the sea, whose waves roared: The Lord of hosts is his name.
>
> And I have put my words in thy mouth, and I have covered thee in the shadow of mine hand, that I may plant the heavens, and lay the foundations of the earth, and say unto Zion, Thou art my people. (Isaiah 51:9–13, 15–16.)

I love this scripture for its generous and loving spirit. The Lord is not grudging or judgmental or threatening. He is eager to protect us, to remind us of our own strength, and to remind us that all of his strength is also bent toward our protection. When you grow up on an island, the way Ed and I did, you don't underestimate the power of the sea. We know something about the churning of the sea and the roaring of its waves. Our power looks like very little compared to the sea. But the sea is nothing to God. He makes it roar and he can make it still. This is the sea that the Lord will dry up so that he can make a smooth road for us to walk on back to his presence, an easy way, a clear way. He will set aside anything and turn any hazard into goodness and mercy for us. May we have the confidence to put our hand in his and move forward with our lives, trusting to his goodness.

Notes

1. Marie K. Hafen, "Celebrating Womanhood," *Ensign*, June 1992, p. 53.

2. Eric Marshall and Stuart Hample, comps., *Children's Letters to God*, enl. ed. (New York: Pocket Books, 1975), not paginated.

3. "Missionaries Assist at Pearl Harbor," *Church News*, 14 December 1991, p. 14.

PART THREE

Gladness and Sadness

8

Rejoice with Joy
and Singing

$\mathcal{I}$saiah 35:1–2 is a beautiful and powerful scripture: "The wilderness and the solitary place shall be glad . . . and the desert shall rejoice, and blossom as the rose. It shall blossom abundantly, and rejoice even with joy and singing . . . they shall see the glory of the Lord, and the excellency of our God."

This scripture prompts our thinking about three concepts: First, what to do in our wilderness and our solitary places of adversity; second, the role of rejoicing in our spiritual lives, and third, seeing "the glory of the Lord and the excellency of our God."

The Wilderness of Adversity

Let's talk about wildernesses of adversity first. I know quite a lot about wilderness, including the Tucson variety, which is a

This address was delivered at the Tucson Region women's conference in Arizona, 12 September 1992.

desert type of wilderness. You might think that a person from Hawaii doesn't know much about living in a desert, but you'd be wrong! I lived on the desert side of the big island of Hawaii. We had lots of cactus and mesquite trees. We used to eat the cactus fruit and feed the mesquite beans to our pigs. I still remember how things would spring unexpectedly alive when it rained (which was seldom). We didn't have grass or lawns. Deserts don't. I remember, one year when I was about seven, a storm made things burst into sudden life; and one of those explosions was a patch of dandelions. My mother was delighted, because new dandelion leaves were tender and spicy to eat. When they were big enough, she told me to go pick the dandelion leaves. I did, but before I started picking I lay down on the bed of dandelions and just rolled back and forth. They were so soft, and felt so luxurious!

So even a desert has its luxuriant moments and its gentle side! But these moments come after a long and patient wait. The other thing we know about a wilderness is that it's a very good place to find God. Moses found a burning bush in his wilderness. Jesus found angels who ministered to him after he was weak from forty days of fasting and after he had been tempted three times. And the Latter-day Saints found Zion when they followed their prophet into the wilderness.

But what do we do with our personal wildernesses, our bleak and desolate times when we feel overwhelmed by the needs around us and by our own inadequacies? What do we do when we feel parched by sorrow and hopelessness, as if our best efforts are of no use?

I love a story that Suzanne Evertsen Lundquist told at BYU Women's Conference: "Just prior to my divorce, I was driving to work on a brittle winter day. My [six] children were suffering; my soul could not be comforted. I cried unto the Lord. 'I don't want to be tried; I don't want to be a God. All I want is a complete, righteous family.' The Lord quickly responded, . . . 'That is all I want.'"[1]

In a system that gives everyone freedom, there are seldom quick or easy solutions to anything. Instead, we have to learn to make progress slowly, sometimes measuring it by inches. Many of you in this audience are experienced in grief. You have lost a loved one to death or to distance or to divorce. You have learned the lessons of living with loss that I am learning now as a recent widow. It would be wrong to creep away with my grief and consider my life over because Ed is gone; but at the same time, it would be wrong to lay upon myself the burden of hiding my feelings and pretending that this loss was not important. In situations like this, we need to be patient with ourselves and do the best we can with what we have.

Patience is a worthy and fruitful approach to a great many problems. I love a poem by Carol Lynn Pearson called "Creation Continued," because she talks about many of the little wildernesses that we face as women and what we can do about it. She writes:

> I will continue
> To create the universe today
> Right where God left off.
>
> Little pockets of chaos
> Somehow survived the ordering
> And I feel moved
> To move upon them
> As in the beginning
> The Spirit of God moved
> Upon the face of the waters.
>
> I will move upon my backyard today
> And the weeds will be subdued
> And the flowers can grow
> And it will be good.
>
> I will move long-distance
> Upon a broken heart
> And leave a little balm
> And it will be good.
>
> I will move upon the hunger of my children
> With salad and spaghetti
> Which is Emily's favorite

And it will be good
And even they will say so.
And I will move too
Upon their minds,
Leaving a little poem
Or an important thought
And that will be even better
Though they won't say so.

I will move upon
Birth defects and AIDS
With five and ten dollar checks
To help the scientists
Who are battling the big chaos
And I will move upon world hunger
With a twenty-four dollar check
For little Marilza in Brazil
And it will be good.

I will move upon
The kitchen floor
And the dirty laundry
And a blank piece of paper
And at the end of the day
Have a little creation to show.

And the evening and the morning
Are my eighteen thousand
and ninety-sixth day
And tomorrow will start another one.
And here is chaos and there is chaos
And who knows if creation
Will finally be done?[2]

The wilderness of affliction calls us to be patient and to continue the work of creation with the means that we have at our disposal, with faith that the blossoms will come. And this is the way the gospel itself works. President Ezra Taft Benson, speaking at the October 1985 general conference, said: "The

Lord works from the inside out. The world works from the outside in. The world would take people out of the slums. Christ takes the slums out of people, and then they take themselves out of the slums. The world would mold [people] by changing their environment. Christ changes [people] who then change their environment. The world would shape human behavior, but Christ can change human nature."[3]

Often it's very hard to endure pain, even if we know it will lessen a little each day. Often it's hard for us to feed only one hungry child when we know there are hundreds and even thousands of children who go to bed hungry. Sometimes we aren't patient with our own achievements. Sister Laural Thatcher Ulrich, the first LDS woman to win a Pulitzer Prize, gave the commencement address at the University of Utah in the spring of 1991. She won that prize—and by the way, she loaned it to the Museum of Church History and Art as part of the Relief Society centennial exhibit—for her biography of Martha Ballard, an eighteenth-century midwife and diarist in New England. Laurel has also won the Bollinger Prize for History and the MacArthur Fellowship, which comes with a no-strings grant of $320,000.

Now, you need to understand that she had been one of the valedictorians of her graduating class thirty-two years earlier at the University of Utah. She was a young married woman, pregnant with her first child; and she and her husband, Gael, went to Boston, where he went to school. Laurel was active in the Church, raised five children, was one of the founding editors of *Exponent II*, and slowly discovered her deep and abiding love of history.

I think that, perhaps because she had had the experience of being a mother and tending a house and garden, she saw things in Martha Ballard's diary that the male historians who had looked at it earlier and dismissed it as not very important had overlooked. Perhaps that's one reason why she did such profoundly significant work and why these honors and prizes flowed to her. She found her own voice, and she gave us back the voices of women who have been largely silenced by their cultures. Then she said—and this is the point about patience I wanted you to pay attention to:

> . . . I am grateful that 32 years ago, I earned both a Phi Beta Kappa key and a safety pin, and that for the past twenty years I have been able to combine motherhood with "a practical life-work." My children's lives have been enriched by my scholarship, and my scholarship has been enriched by my life as a housewife and mother. When people ask me how I have done it, I usually say, "A little at a time."

That's a gentle answer, isn't it? Laurel smiled when she said it, and so did most of the women in the audience. I think it's great to do things a little at a time when you're also giving your time to other things that are important to you, such as your family and your Church responsibilities. Laurel explained: "It took me five years to complete a one year M.A., nine to do a Ph.D., eight years to write Martha Ballard's book. Meanwhile Gael and I *together* raised our children."[4]

Laurel is someone who looked at a situation that could have been a desert and instead grew a garden. Her situation reminds me of another characteristic of a wilderness. It is actually, for all its desolation, a very fertile place, but it is fertile in its own way, on its own schedule, according to its own timetable. The seeds lie dormant for many weeks, sometimes many months, waiting for conditions to be right. But when their opportunity comes, they know what to do to seize it, and the desert blossoms as the rose.

Isaiah also speaks to this condition of patience when he tells us to wait and help each other to wait: "Strengthen ye the weak hands, and confirm the feeble knees. Say to them that are of a fearful heart, Be strong, fear not: behold, your God will come . . . he will come and save you." (Isaiah 35:3–4.)

So in your own moments of wilderness, I ask you to remember two things: Think of Carol Lynn's poem and do what you can about the "pockets of chaos" that lie within your power to do something about. And second, remember Laurel and give yourself permission to achieve great things a little at a time.

The Role of Rejoicing

We've talked a little about what to do when we find ourselves in the wilderness of our affliction. The second point I
want to make is the role of rejoicing in our spiritual lives. The
gospel is the good news of Jesus Christ, but sometimes we act as
if we think it's bad news. We feel anxious and guilty, burdened
and exhausted. I'm here today to testify of the good news of the
Savior's inexhaustible love for each one of us. For me, for you.
Jesus Christ agreed to come to the earth and become our Savior
long before he knew whether you were going to do genealogical
work on Tuesday or keep a spotless house or have eight children
or memorize quotations out of the *Ensign*. He suffered in Geth-
semane and died on the cross, not so that we could keep our
Righteousness Checklists better but so that we could "have life,
and . . . have it more abundantly" (John 10:10). Jesus knows all
of our faults and shortcomings as well as all of our talents and
achievements and good intentions. He accepts us and loves us
beyond our understanding. The Apostle Paul promised:

> we are more than conquerors through him that loved us.
> For I am persuaded, that neither death, nor life, nor angels,
> nor principalities, nor powers, nor things present, nor things to
> come,
> Nor height, nor depth, nor any other creature, shall be able
> to separate us from the love of God, which is in Christ Jesus our
> Lord. (Romans 8:37–39.)

Let me read that again with some more details, the way Paul
might have said it if he were talking to the women in the
Church today:

> For I am persuaded, that neither death, nor life, nor angels,
> nor principalities, nor powers, nor divorce, nor widowhood, nor
> children gone astray, nor infertility, nor little shortcomings, nor
> major mistakes, nor poverty, nor lack of education, nor too much
> education, nor illness, nor sexual abuse, nor incest, nor single-
> ness, nor insensitive leaders, nor gossip, nor spite, nor prejudice,

nor feelings of guilt, nor feelings of inadequacy, nor loneliness, nor sorrow, nor pain, nor any other creature, shall be able to separate us from the love of God, which is in Christ Jesus our Lord.

My feeling is that when we feel that inexhaustible love springing up in our hearts, acts of service and mercy and kindness will flow from us. We don't need to force ourselves. We don't need to berate ourselves for not doing better. We don't need to compare ourselves to anyone else. We are okay, just the way we are, each of us, with our own needs, our own abilities, our own desires for righteousness, and our own set of obstacles to overcome and our own contributions—whether large or small—to make.

I think that no one leads a life of unremitting happiness. We probably wouldn't enjoy it if we did. But I think some people have the spiritual strength and serenity to come very close to always having the Holy Ghost with them, to always feeling the sweet influence and closeness of the Savior. These people have a strong sense of their spiritual identity, and they have a strong awareness of their Heavenly Father's love.

I want to tell you about a woman who I think exemplifies this principle. She wasn't a Mormon. In fact, she wasn't a Christian. She was a Jew, a concentration camp survivor. Counselor Paul Pearsall was struck by the contrast between her laughter and the purple numbers tattooed on her wrist. He marveled at her resilience: "She had been tortured, seen her own parents and [all but two] of her relatives killed, and had lived in the agony, squalor, and starvation of a prison camp for most of the young years of her life. She was within days of being killed when the camp was liberated. She had every reason to be weak, bitter, sick, and depressed. Instead, she was one of the most joyful, hardiest women I have ever met."

She laughed, sang, played with the children, created mischief, and stirred up excitement wherever she went. She teased her son and daughter-in-law for being "moping, dreadfully distracted people too busy to visit a crazy old lady." They wished she would settle down and act her age. In this counselor's opinion, they should be "learning from her instead of trying to cope with her."

One day Claire caught Paul Pearsall looking at the tattoo on her wrist. She confided that she thought of it as a constant reminder "to live and to love. To me, it could be a heart instead of a number."

What were the lessons that Claire learned from her terrible ordeal? One of the most important was free agency. She watched the prisoners who stayed reasonably healthy and noticed that their strength came, initially, from pretending to be strong. "Then they actually became strong. We were all afraid, but we learned to change our feelings by acting. Those were the people I copied. The strong ones. . . . There came a time when you had to decide not to surrender but to accept, to get involved in the experience, and to change it from the inside. When you did that, you went outside the walls."

A second lesson was service. What kind of service could a concentration camp prisoner render? Claire found a way. Every evening, she'd share a bit of her inadequate ration with one of the guard dogs. When an inmate asked her why, she would say, "For life, for hope, for staying alive. The dog doesn't choose to be here either. He's a prisoner of this cruelty too. When I feed him, it's as if I send a message that we will all survive and take care of each other."

She also found someone who needed her human sympathy, a man so terrorized by the prison camp experience that he would "shake terribly" as the guards held roll call. Claire would quietly hold his hand. She observed, "He said it gave him strength, but it seemed to give me more strength. I seemed to get some type of energy from calming him, from comforting him."[5]

This woman understood the role of rejoicing in her spiritual life. She wasn't sitting passively waiting for everything to become perfect, and she wasn't scurrying around anxiously trying to make everything—including herself—perfect. She did just what she could with the resources she had: a little piece of bread for a dog, holding the hand of a frightened human being, and finding strength in herself. When you feel heavy laden, will you remember Claire and lighten up?

Maren Mouritsen told the women at BYU's women's conference about her mother who had suffered "a series of debilitating strokes that left her completely paralyzed on the left side, and without speech." When Maren was home for the summer after her first year at college, she and her father would get her mother ready for church, go to choir practice, and then walk back to get her before Sunday School. (They lived near the chapel.) Then one Sunday, Maren went back for her mother and discovered that she "had rolled out the front door and onto the ramp that we had built shortly after she became ill. There was the wheelchair and my mother—smack dab in the middle of the zinnias and the pansies. Fearing the worst, I hurried to her side, only to find her propped up against the wall. With her only good hand she had written in the dirt, 'Flowers pretty.' I thought to myself, 'Woman beautiful.'"[6]

Isaiah understands the role of rejoicing in our spiritual lives. In chapter 35, after talking about strengthening the weak hands and confirming the feeble knees and promising that God will come to save us, he bursts into this glorious psalm of rejoicing:

> Then the eyes of the blind shall be opened, and the ears of the deaf shall be unstopped.
>
> Then shall the lame man leap as an hart, and the tongue of the dumb sing: for in the wilderness shall waters break out, and streams in the desert.
>
> And the parched ground shall become a pool, and the thirsty land springs of water: in the habitation of dragons, where each lay, shall be grass with reeds and rushes. (Isaiah 35:5–7.)

Seeing the Glory of the Lord

We've talked about what to do in the wilderness of our affliction and our power to choose rejoicing in our spiritual lives—the blossoming of our desert. The third point Isaiah mentions is: "They shall see the glory of the Lord and the excellency of our God" (Isaiah 35:2).

As desert dwellers, you know that there are some beauties peculiar to the wilderness that are sometimes hard for others to see. I'm thinking of the certain slants of light, the size of the sky, the sweep of the cloud, the shape and ripples of the sand dunes, the color and textures of its tough plants. All of these are desert beauties that someone trained to see the beauty of the Florida Everglades or the Olympic rain forest may not notice for years.

It's the same with seeing the glory of Lord. There are times when this glory is all around us and we wonder how anyone could miss seeing it. And then there are times when we have to search for the glory. You know, I think both times are all right—all right with God and all right for us to experience. One of my favorite books is *Children's Letters to God,* a compilation of the questions young children, probably in the second and third grade, asked God. I love their candor and their freshness and honesty. Listen to these letters and think about how these children relate to God:

> Dear God, are you real? Some people don't believe it. If you are you better do something quick. Harriet Ann

> Dear God, I have pictures of all the leaders except you. Norman

> I'm sorry I did not write before but I only learned how this week. Martha

> Dear God, If I was God I wouldn't be as good at it. Keep it up. Michelle

> Dear God, I didn't think orange went very good with purple until I saw the sunset you made on Tue[sday]. That was cool. Eugene

And this last one:

> Dear God, Count me in. Your friend, Herbie.[7]

I think there may be more real praise, real communication, real worship, and real theological struggling in some of these one-sentence letters than we sometimes get in a whole Sunday

School class. Somehow we get the message that Heavenly Father doesn't want the real us. He wants the prettied-up us, the does-everything-right us, the almost-perfect us. Sometimes we believe that Jesus is saying, "Clean up your act and then come back." He wants us just as we are—broken, feeble, imperfect, limited in understanding, and limited in achievement. Listen to what he says:

> Let not your heart be troubled: ye believe in God, believe also in me.
>
> In my Father's house are many mansions: if it were not so, I would have told you. I go to prepare a place for you.
>
> And if I go and prepare a place for you, I will come again, and receive you unto myself; that where I am, there ye may be also.
>
> And whither I go ye know, and the way ye know.
>
> Thomas saith unto him, Lord, we know not whither thou goest; and how can we know the way?
>
> Jesus saith unto him, I am the way, the truth, and the life: no man cometh unto the Father, but by me. (John 14:1–6.)

We don't have to bulldoze our way up a mountain to get to him or hack our way through a jungle or walk across the burning desert to come to him. He comes to us and receives us to himself and makes the way for us by which we can come. In fact, the Savior *is* the way. We can find him in purple sunsets, in our questions, and in our imperfections, because he is there with us. Through his infinite sacrifice, he has already counted us in.

And let us look for the Savior in the eyes and faces of those around us. Mother Teresa said that she chose her life of service with the poor of Calcutta because, she said, "[I] felt that God wanted from me something more. He wanted me to be poor with the poor and to love him in the distressing disguise of the poorest of the poor."[8] Jesus tells us that each person in need is the Savior in disguise—"Inasmuch as ye have done it unto one of the least of these my brethren [or sisters], ye have done it unto me" (Matthew 25:40). Some of these disguises are the delightful disguises of our own children's beautiful faces, or the loving, gentle faces of our own parents and spouses. Sometimes they are the distressing and painful disguises of the homeless, the healthless, the hopeless. But when we see the Savior in such a disguise, then we are truly seeing the glory of the Lord, for our work is the same as his—"to bring to pass the immortality and eternal life" of all human beings, beginning with ourselves and with the people who are closest to us (Moses 1:39).

Let us remember one more fact about a desert. Even if the seeds are ready, they can't make it rain. The rain comes through the mercy and charity and compassion of our Heavenly Father. Are there people around you who need a little mercy and charity before they can blossom? Is it possible that Heavenly Father wants you to provide that life-giving change in their environment so they can blossom as the rose? I hope so.

Conclusion

Think again of being in the desert—hot, dry, thirsty, with the sun beating down on you, and thirst making your mouth dry. We can't always sweep through the wilderness in air-conditioned comfort with a cold drink from 7-Eleven on the dashboard. Sometimes we have to plod slowly and steadily toward our goal. Sometimes we have to hunger and thirst for righteousness. Sometimes we have to pursue our goals a little at a time, as Laurel did. Sometimes, after a long wait, the desert bursts into bloom of itself, but at other times we have to plant the seeds, and carry water and stand by with a sunshade, too! But blossom it will.

Remember the women we have talked about. Remember Carol Lynn and the wisdom of finding the little ways in which we can move upon the chaos close to us. Remember Laurel's patience, and be willing to achieve great things a little at a time.

Remember the role of rejoicing in our spiritual lives. Think of Claire sharing her pitiful ration of bread with a guard dog. Think of the feelings you have at this moment, and lighten up on yourself and on others. Let us find the real joy of knowing that Jesus is our yokefellow in the tasks we must face. Remember Mother Teresa, who sees the face of Jesus in the faces of those she serves. "The glory of the Lord and the excellency of our God" is all around us—in the world that he has created for us, in the faces of others, and in ourselves. Isaiah promises us:

> And an highway shall be there, and a way, and it shall be called The way of holiness; the unclean shall not pass over it; but it shall be for those: the wayfaring men, though fools, shall not err therein.
>
> No lion shall be there, nor any ravenous beast shall go up thereon, it shall not be found there; but the redeemed shall walk there:
>
> And the ransomed of the Lord shall return, and come to Zion with songs and everlasting joy upon their heads: they shall obtain joy and gladness, and sorrow and sighing shall flee away. (Isaiah 35:8–10.)

We know the way. Jesus said, "I am the way." Let us follow him, rejoicing, and enter Zion with singing.

Notes

1. "The Repentance of Eve," in *As Women of Faith: Talks Selected from the BYU Women's Conferences*, edited by Mary E. Stovall and Carol Cornwall Madsen (Salt Lake City: Deseret Book Company, 1989), p. 101.

2. *Women I Have Known and Been*, (Salt Lake City, Aspen Books, 1992), pp. 2–3. Copyright by Carol Lynn Pearson. Used by permission.

3. In "Born of God," *Ensign*, November 1985, p. 6.

4. Laurel Thatcher Ulrich, "A Phi Beta Kappa Key and a Safety Pin," commencement address, University of Utah, 12 June 1992. In *Exponent II*, vol. 17, no. 1, 1992, p. 19.

5. Paul Pearsall, *Super Joy: In Love with Living*, (New York: Doubleday, 1988), pp. 1, 8–9, 11, 22, 19–20.

6. Maren Mouritsen, *"There's a Horse in the House,"* BYU Today, July 1992, p. 42.

7. Eric Marshall and Stuart Hample, comps., *Children's Letters to God*, enl. ed. (New York: Pocket Books, 1975), not paginated.

8. José Luis González-Balado and Janet N. Playfoot, *My Life for the Poor: Mother Teresa of Calcutta* (San Francisco: Harper & Row, Publishers, 1985), p. 6.

9

Spunk, Sunshine, and Survival

*L*ike many others, I'm a cancer survivor. I had a radical mastectomy in 1973 and a hysterectomy three months later. I know what it is like to not take my body for granted, to be health-conscious, but also to know that there may not be too much I can do about it. I have to watch my cholesterol. I have a tricky arthritis condition that I control by watching my diet really closely. What's the recipe when life hands you a death sentence? Spunk, sunshine, and survival. But the funny thing about that death sentence—or life sentence—is that everybody, even little babies in strollers, are under the same death sentence. It's called life! So here we are, alive, making choices for life, and facing death. But we're the lucky ones. We're the survivors, and we know how to bring sunshine into our lives. We know how to meet problems with spunk and sunshine. The unlucky ones are the people out there who believe nothing will

The original version of this address was read for me by Carol Lee Hawkins of the Relief Society General Board at a tri-stake health fair in Delta, Utah, on 21 March 1992, while my husband was dying. Gary Stay was the administrator of the local hospital and organizer of the conference.

happen to them. Among them are the women who don't take seriously the risks—that one in nine will have breast cancer. They're the 60 percent of women at risk in this county who haven't had the screening yet.

When I discovered a lump in my breast, the biopsy and the mastectomy were done in the same operation, followed by several weeks of radiation therapy. When they wheeled me back to my room after surgery, and I groggily opened my eyes, the two faces that swam into focus at the foot of my bed were those of my husband, Ed, and Laura Stay, Gary's wife. How can I thank her for her support and comforting love during a time of trial for me!

During my recuperation, for about six weeks part of my physical therapy was a child's toy—a little rubber ball attached by an elastic to a paddle. This exercise was to build up the muscles under my arm where they'd been removed. I also practiced squeezing a ball in my hands. And another exercise was spider-walking my fingers up the wall three times a day—morning, noon, and night—with the goal of getting my hand above my head. I didn't know if I'd ever be able to lift my arm above my head. I remember trying to spider-walk on the wall and feeling that my arm was a dead weight that was no longer connected to my brain. I'd stretch and stretch to get my middle fingernail even a fraction of an inch higher, and then mark where I had to stop. I cheered for myself when there was even the slightest progress. And when there was none, I'd console myself by thinking, "That's okay; just wait until I try it again at noon." That's what I call being spunky; never giving up, celebrating even a fraction of an inch. At the end of six weeks, I could get my arm up above my head. And now I can lift anything, turn it in any direction, move without thinking about it.

The cancer wasn't through with me at that point, though. That same year, my Pap smear showed the presence of some irregular cells, and a biopsy confirmed it. So I had a hysterectomy three months later. Then in 1986, thirteen years later, I noticed a pin-point lesion on my chest. I watched it closely for a few days, and it got larger. I went in again to my doctor. Again it was malignant. Again there was an operation, and again there was radiation therapy. The amazing thing to me was that, even after thirteen years, my original X-rays were still in the lab, wedged in the back of a filing cabinet and found by a technician who felt a prompting to keep searching. Thus, we were able to determine that the malignancy had recurred in the intersection between two areas that should have overlapped in the first radiation but which had not, leaving a tiny zone that had not been irradiated. It meant that there was a reasonable explanation for the recurrence. It also meant that I needed a very minimal amount of radiation this second time. I went in every morning at six for treatment and was still at my school by seven-thirty. There has been no identifiable recurrence since that time.

But what of my future? Since there's no known cause of breast cancer, there's no known prevention. I live one day at a time, like you, with spunk, finding as much sunshine as I can. Whether we're dealing with osteoporosis, diabetes, cancer, PMS, or some other chronic condition, that's all we can do. And whether our conditions are terminal or not, so far, we're all survivors. I'd like to share with you some guidelines about how to survive with spunk and sunshine.

First, keep a positive mental attitude. I'm talking about this part first, because it was fairly easy for me. The doctor had talked to both Ed and me about some of the psychological side effects of cancer, so Ed was very aware of my moods and feelings. He could not have been more supportive. I knew that he would have instantly taken the cancer upon himself, if that had been possible, because his love for me was so great. He never talked about his own worries; he was always so cheerful and so appreciative and so supportive that it was a lift to my spirits to be around him.

Ed and I have very similar personalities, so this approach was a great strength to me. But this may not always be the case. In your circumstances, you may need to talk about your fears or you may need to have worries shared with you, otherwise it may seem to you that you are being asked to pretend that everything is all right so that your spouse and your children will not worry.

Or you may feel that your husband doesn't want to know how you feel as you move through the process and that he just wants things "fixed" so that the time of uncertainty will end. There are support groups and counselors who can help then; but I think it's essential that a good relationship not be a casualty of cancer.

I was lucky, perhaps because I'd had some training in looking at difficult situations earlier in my life. I didn't waste time or energy denying or resisting the fact that I had cancer, that I had a mastectomy, and that I had a hysterectomy. I didn't grieve. I just said, "It's one of those things I can overcome." My doctor said, "It's easy to treat you, because I don't also have to treat you psychologically." I don't want to imply by that that he was only interested in how my body was responding. He was a very caring individual. But by that I think he meant that he and I were both focusing our energies on the same goal so a lot of roadblocks that could have slowed the process down just didn't get set up. I felt blessed that the doctors could do something and that the prognosis was good. I weighed the good and the bad and decided that there was more good than bad. I felt I couldn't dwell on it, and I didn't.

Now, I realize it's easier to say things like this than it is to do it. I also realize that everyone is different. You're an individual. You have your own pace, your own way of coping, your own style of acceptance. But I think we all agree that you can't deal with reality by denying it, so accepting the facts and moving on quickly seems to be the healthiest approach. Find the good in your situation and be positive about it.

This takes a lot of creativity, as you might imagine; but I think the ultimate expression of a positive mental attitude was Missy Cannel's column in the *Salt Lake Tribune* on August 10, 1990. She called breast cancer "My Life Enhancer." Now *that*, I thought when I read it, is a title that grabs your attention! For her cancer was a year-long saga of having a bilateral mastectomy, chemotherapy, and reconstructive surgery. She met this ordeal as an opportunity. Six years earlier, she'd decided to listen to the "inner voice screaming at me to take control," so she had stopped smoking, started exercising, and begun working on her motivation. She decided to treat her cancer as a "chance to test my new and improved coping skills" and "use this time for some personal growth."

She decided that she was not going to lose her hair and she was not going to be nauseated. She also decided that she needed a really big project to absorb her attention and keep it focused away from the treatments, so she remodeled the house.

> The kitchen was the biggest project, as we totally gutted it. Next was the bedroom. Out with the dark wood and in with a bright white lacquer bedroom set. Now that these two rooms were finished, I was outside to work in the yard. I did much digging in the dirt and even more digging into my inner self. It was a quiet time of introspecting and was very healing. As chemo ends, so do my projects, and I have a beautiful new me that I know better and a beautiful house and yard in which to live my "new life."

This isn't all, of course. Missy has been involved in several outreach efforts, helping other women, working in a support group, and contributing a chapter to a book. When she says cancer was a life-enhancer for her, she means it. This proves it, and it sets a high standard for the rest of us.

So the first suggestion I have is to keep a positive attitude, not just in the first days after the discovery, or the first weeks of treatment, or the first months of recovery, but continually. You might have to manufacture sunshine for a while, or even import it, but keep it in your life.

My second suggestion for surviving with spunk and sunshine is to let others share your experience. In those three days between my discovery of the lump and the operation, Ed and I talked only to each other. One of our sons was in Brazil, serving an LDS mission. The other was at college. My mother was in California, living with my brother and sister-in-law and caring for their children while they worked. I knew that all of them would be concerned and worried, but there was literally nothing they could do at that stage besides worry with us—and Ed and I weren't immersed in worrying. We knew that we would need to

share the information widely as soon as we knew what the diag-
nosis was, and we were willing to do that, but those three days
were a quiet space for us, a time for us to gather our own
strength and to strengthen each other. If we had begun calling—telling friends and neighbors and family—then we would
have had to process the shock, the worry, and the concern with
each person. And even though their love and concern would
have been encouraging and supportive, we were still processing
the news ourselves. It seemed better for us to wait.

Your circumstances may be different. I know that for some
women, sharing the news with a circle of friends and family
helps them to accept the facts more quickly themselves. Sometimes being able to draw on the support and sympathy are encouraging in the face of fears and doubts.

Of course, as soon as we knew from the biopsy that it *was*
cancer, then we called Bob at school, told my mother, and
wrote a letter to Ken in Brazil. In Ken's case, it almost backfired.
One of the women in the ward had a daughter in Ken's mission,
and *her* letter was delivered to her daughter before ours was delivered to Ken, so she was expressing her sympathy before Ken
knew there was anything wrong. *Then* he worried. His letter and
ours crossed in the mail, and as soon as we received his, we tele-
phoned him, too.

Ken's reaction made me aware of something else. There are
some people who have earned the right to worry with you even
during the few days of uncertainty. Of course, there's nothing
they can actually do, any more than there's anything you can
actually do. But they can be with you, psychologically and spiritually, while you are in this state of uncertainty and anxiety.
You're not asking them to fix anything by telling them; you're
saying, "You are so close to me that you are part of this experience, too." For most of us, that's our families. But there are also
special friends who have that right.

Sometimes people aren't quite sure how to express their support and you're not quite sure how to let them. My operation
was quite a while ago, you know, where people were much less
open about cancer. And breast cancer particularly lay in the

category of "embarrassing" diseases. I'm certainly glad that's changing! A lot of women are dead because they were too "embarrassed" to do something about it.

I'll never forget, though, when some of my teachers came to visit me in the hospital for the first time. I knew how they were going to feel. They would be shocked, worried, afraid of hurting my feelings, uncomfortable, and not quite sure what to do. So I decided, "It's up to me to show them that I'm still me—that the cancer isn't me and that it hasn't changed me."

I was resting in my bed, not asleep but with my eyes closed, when I heard footsteps in the hall and some whispering. My door was open and I could just see Beth's head as she peeked around the corner of the door. I smiled and waved and called, "Beth, what are you hiding out there in the hall for? C'mon in. And I know that Evelyn and Mary are with you, too! Come in and I'll tell you all about it."

So they came in, looking anxious and embarrassed but also relieved. I didn't let it stop there. I said, "Well, aren't you going to ask me what happened?" And I told them the whole story, and in a few minutes we were all laughing together. That first meeting was important, because they enjoyed the visit and went back to the school to tell the other teachers that I was fine. I hadn't become the disease, and I hadn't let cancer change me into someone else. I was still the person they had known.

This wasn't easy. I was used to being very active, to figuring out how to solve problems and then doing it. I'd always been very energetic and fast moving. I'd been healthy during the pregnancies and bounced back quickly after the boys were born, so I was used to taking my body for granted—assuming that it would do whatever I needed to have done. The surgery was a big adjustment and so was the radiation therapy. I was physically weak and had to get used to myself in a whole new way. There was so much that I had to leave to the Lord. I knew that I must not let this time of physical weakness become a time of spiritual weakness as well. I learned to accept each day, just as it came, and find joy in whatever moments it brought me.

I was blessed with a wonderful friend during this period—

Louise Erickson, who was in our Relief Society presidency. She knew just how to help me. She drove me every day to the radiation therapy, called me on the phone, and made sure that I did not worry about household things.

Many times when people help us we have no way to return our thanks directly and must be contented with helping someone else in need. But Louise understood how important it was to me to give, even while I was receiving so very much from her. She was making a pretty yellow and green afghan out of squares hooked on a little frame. Now, crocheting is not exactly a Japanese art, but she patiently taught me how to do the pattern. It was a simple pattern, so that in just a half hour I could make a square. My, how I enjoyed that! Even when I didn't feel like getting out of bed and sometimes felt too weak to concentrate on reading, I could still make a square and enjoy that little achievement. What a great friend Louise was! She not only gave me the essential service that my body needed while it healed but she also gave me the service that my soul needed. I hope that when these experiences come to you, you have a Louise.

My third suggestion for surviving with spunk and sunshine is to keep your sense of perspective. A good laugh is worth a lot of philosophizing. When I think of perspective, I think of one of my favorite Calvin and Hobbes cartoons. I wouldn't say that Calvin is a typical first-grader, but he certainly has the spunk and energy of one. And everybody needs a friend with the loyalty of his stuffed tiger, Hobbes.

In this cartoon, Calvin and Hobbes are walking through the woods on their way home and Calvin is holding forth grandly. "I believe history is a force. Its unalterable tide sweeps all people and institutions along its unrelenting path. Everything and everyone serves history's single purpose."

Hobbes, looking puzzled, inquires, "And what is that purpose?"

"Why, to produce *me*, of course!" explains Calvin. "I'm the end result of history. . . . Think of it! Thousands of generations lived and died to produce my exact, specific parents, whose reason for being, obviously, was to produce me. All history up to this point has been spent preparing the world for my presence."

"Hmm," observes Hobbes. "Four and a half billion years probably wasn't long enough."

"Now I'm here," announces Calvin, posing on top of a boulder, "and history is vindicated."

"So now that history's brought you," asks Hobbes, "what are you going to do?"

The last frame shows them both sitting in front of the TV.[1]

Well, that kind of says where we can all end up, doesn't it, even if we do have those wonderful moments of feeling that, yes, the whole point of history *was* to produce us. So what I'm suggesting is that we keep perspective in our lives.

And one of the best ways we can keep perspective in our lives is to follow the instructions in Okazaki chapter one, verse one and lighten up! When we have the power within ourselves to not take ourselves so seriously and not take seriously the burdens that life heaps upon us, we not only have fewer burdens but we can handle those we have more gracefully and graciously. You've all heard how Norman Cousins used to watch old television comedies when he was sick. He said that if he could get in a good laugh, he would rest more soundly than if he had a sleeping pill. So keep the sunshine in your life. What tickles your funny bone? Keep it tickled during these times. Collect cartoons. Watch a kitten.

Now, my real test about keeping my perspective was in adjusting to the prosthesis. It took a long time before it felt natural and comfortable. It was hard to remember to check myself in the mirror every morning to see if I was lopsided. And having a missing breast is a complicated social and emotional thing. If someone was in a wheelchair, you wouldn't feel at all constrained about thinking, "Oh, a handicapped person," or talking to that person and maybe even asking what happened, how they're getting along, and how you can help. But can you imagine walking up to someone and saying, "Oh, I see that you have a missing breast. Tell me about it."

I was self-conscious about my changed appearance for several months, but what really pushed me into acceptance was how *funny* my prosthesis was. I liked to swim—that's what I did for exercise—and for months I tried to swim with that silly prosthesis. It kept rubbing and slipping sideways because of the overhead arm motion. I became really irritated trying to keep it adjusted. And the final straw was one morning when I suddenly realized it was missing. I was splashing around in the pool thinking, "Now where did that blasted thing go?" And there it was, on the bottom of the pool. I dived down to get it and said to myself, "I've *had* it! I'm never going to do this again. I'm here to swim, not to show off my body." So when I got home, I told Ed what happened, we laughed together, and I bought a lovely Spandex suit that made me feel I was slipping through the water like a dolphin. After that, I just concentrated on enjoying swimming.

I think you all know what I'm talking about. Our perspective inevitably alters when we have a chronic illness or cancer. It can be terrifying to realize that our body is letting us down. We've lived inside this collection of muscles and organs and bones since before we can remember, and we feel betrayed when it gets sick, when it lets cancer cells start taking over. We have to work out a newer, more complicated relationship with our bodies and this means getting in touch with needs we may never have realized we had. This process becomes urgently important when we are facing a chronic or terminal illness, because it reminds us that our time is limited.

Some of you may feel terribly trapped in your body because you have a genetic disease or because other people in your family have cancer and you know that the risk goes up for you, too. I want to read you a statement that I think is very encouraging.

You do not have to be your mother unless she is who you want to be. You do not have be your mother's mother, or your mother's mother's mother. . . . You may inherit their chins or their hips or their eyes, but you are not destined to become the women who came before you. You are not destined to live their lives. . . . Inherit their strength. If you inherit something, inherit their resilience. Because the only person you are destined to become is the person you decide to be. The body you have is the body you inherited, but you must decide what to do with it. . . . So thank your mother for what you happened to be born with, but thank yourself for what you actually do with it. (Nike advertisement.)

Now, *that's* a healthy perspective!

My fourth suggestion is to assign meaning to your life, and let it be a loving meaning. Many of you may be Latter-day Saints like me, but others of you have other religious faiths and some of you may have private belief systems instead. Whatever you draw from your religious tradition, you have to evaluate your life for yourself and decide what it means to you. Remember that there are some questions that we simply don't have answers to yet.

One of my favorite books is the delightful collection of children's letters to God. One of these letters was a very good question from a little girl named Jane. She asked, "Instead of letting people die and having to make new ones why don't you just keep the ones you got now?"[2] Well, your religious faith may supply an answer to that question, or maybe you're just as puzzled by it as Jane.

Leah de Roulet, a social worker who counsels terminal cancer patients and their families, spends her days and nights with people "facing the ends of their lives." They ask, "in an urgent and profound way, 'What has *my* life meant.'" As she has gone through the process with them, she's come to the conclusion that love is the purpose. The real reason we exist, she says, "is to somehow enhance each other's humanity." She thinks that the whole meaning of an individual's life eventually focuses on one great question: "How well have I loved? A person can then find hope in believing: Somebody loved me, and I loved him or her and those memories that my loved one carried forward will shimmer on inside my children and grandchildren and beyond." As a professional, she spends a lot of time with elderly people during the closing days of their lives. She finds out that they don't regret being poor or unknown. Instead, their only real worry is "the kinds of things they didn't do and should have done with the people that they loved." We usually think of our families, and most of us have them. But Leah specifically mentioned the richness she felt in the life of a dying woman who had never married because, as a teacher, she said, "'I know I've touched other people's lives and their lives are better for having known me.'" Another of her patients was a seaman who had never married. Instead of spending his last days feeling sorry for himself, he focused on the many friends he had made over his life and found meaning in the fact that "he had instilled a sense of passion for the experience of life within the souls of the people that he had known."[3]

What do you want your life to mean? You have the power to choose that meaning. I want to urge you to let it be a meaning that includes service. Anne Morrow Lindbergh said: "When one is a stranger to oneself, then one is estranged from others, too. If one is out of touch with oneself, then one cannot touch others."[4] And it works both ways, too. It isn't selfish to strengthen ourselves. It's wise. That means we have the ability to strengthen others. Lloyd D. Newell, delivering a sermon in the Salt Lake Tabernacle, explained this process carefully:

> Our ability to reach out to others directly corresponds with our ability to reach into ourselves. For example, airline flight attendants speak of such service every time a plane leaves the ground. . . . In the same way, lifeguards keep struggling swimmers afloat because they are themselves good swimmers, equipped with their own life preservers and experienced in their own flotation techniques. Similarly, teachers must fill their own minds with knowledge before they can increase their students' understanding. In other words, we are in a position to help others when we have first helped ourselves.
>
> Only as our own best caretaker can we be the kind of caregiver the Savior describes: "Thou shalt love thy neighbor as thyself" (Galatians 5:14). When love of self enhances a love for others, we see what is magical about service. It is a two-way exchange. Parents who build their own emotional muscles have strength to lift a discouraged child. Friends who have goals inspire others to set and achieve goals. Spouses who have forgiven themselves can

more readily forgive their companions. An investment in self becomes a deposit for others—with God-given returns.[5]

Yakov Smirnoff, the comedian, tells a story about Leo Tolstoy. When he was an old man, he planted apple seedlings. His neighbor laughed at him. He wouldn't be around to eat those apples. Tolstoy replied, "Yes, but other people will eat them and they will think of me." Smirnoff comments, "I think that's what we're supposed to do: Leave more than we've found, give more than we've received, love more than we've been loved. And while we're here, we should always rewind the videotapes before returning them to the rental store."[6]

There's one service that everyone at this conference can perform. We're some of the lucky ones here, as I said, because we know about our death sentence. There are other people who should be here from Millard County. Some of them may be your sisters, your mothers, your neighbors, your friends. Some of the service that needs to happen is prevention. We know more now about health. We know more about nutrition. We know more about the effects of exercise. We know how much sooner a mammogram can spot a cell mass than we can feel a lump. Encourage somebody you know who needs these tests to come. Drive them in. Be with them. Talk to them about your experience.

The more you know, the more powerful you become and the more you'll be able to work for prevention. Breast cancer is an epidemic. It obviously needs to become a higher research priority and there needs to be more awareness. If your sister's doctor doesn't recommend a mammogram for her, ask him why not—and ask your sister, too. This is a death-defying act that we can all perform, for ourselves and for each other.

So here we are, all survivors. Let's survive with spunk and sunshine, with grace and gratitude. Let's have a positive attitude. Let's find ways to let others share this experience. Let's keep a good perspective and let the healing effects of laughter radiate through our lives as we come to terms with this new relationship with our bodies. Let's infuse our lives with meaning, and reach out to each other in service.

As a Christian, I feel strongly that Jesus Christ is with us in all of these experiences—not always shielding us from them or always turning aside the effects through the intervention of a miracle, but always, *always* with us as we endure, and struggle, and understand. Whatever your religious affiliation, I know that God wants to support you in this experience that you're having; and I invoke his love to surround us, his steadfastness to give us courage, and his delight in giving us joy.

Notes

1. Bill Watterson, *Scientific Progress Goes "Boink": A Calvin and Hobbes Collection* (Kansas City, MO: Andrews and McMeel Books, 1991), p. 27.

2. Eric Marshall and Stuart Hample, comps., *Children's Letters to God*, enl. ed. (New York: Pocket Books, 1975), not paginated.

3. Untitled statement from unidentified magazine. Clipping in my possession.

4. Anne Morrow Lindbergh, *Gift from the Sea* (New York: Random House, 1955), p. 44.

5. Lloyd D. Newell, "The Spoken Word: Strangers to Ourselves," 12 January 1992 (Salt Lake City: The Church of Jesus Christ of Latter-day Saints, 1992). Leaflet in my possession.

6. Untitled statement from unidentified magazine. Clipping in my possession.

10

Earth Smiles in Flowers

*Y*our theme today is a song of gladness and a cry of triumph in the face of adversities: "The earth smiles in flowers." It reminds me of that luxuriant scripture from the Song of Solomon that captures so fully the joy of spring: "Rise up, my love, my fair one, and come away. For, lo, the winter is past, the rain is over and gone; the flowers appear on the earth; the time of the singing of birds is come, and the voice of the turtle [dove] is heard in our land." (Song of Solomon 2:10–12.)

Let's look at the flowers on the earth of our lives and see how they help us revel in the joy of the gospel during our happy hours and find consolation in it during our sorrowful hours. What do we know about flowers? First, flowers are beautiful in their diversity. In their array of colors and scents they bespeak the divine, inclusive love of our Heavenly Father. Second, they are impermanent, lasting only a short time. Third, they come in their appointed season, in the Lord's due time. Fourth, they do

The original version of this address was presented at a women's conference in the Huntington Beach Region, California, 30 May 1992.

not exist for themselves but to produce fruit and seeds for the future. Now, let's talk about each one of these characteristics of flowers and perhaps feel a flowering in our own hearts of the joy of flowers.

Diversity

The first point I want to make about flowers is that they come in all shapes and sizes, all colors, all scents, and suited to all places. Our diversity is one of the things that God loves about us.

In April 1992 I spent a month in Hawaii, where I toured the stakes for women's conferences and leadership workshops. I was surrounded by flowers. Bougainvillea and hibiscus grew along the streets as we passed. Night-blooming cereus climbed the rocks beside the road. Gardens gloried in orchids and gardenia. Outside the chapel in Laie, plumeria and ginger scented the air. The women to whom I spoke gave me leis of lavender and purple orchids, stephanotis and pikake. One of them looked like a golden fretwork, made of fifteen hundred sweet-scented plumeria petals, stitched with love. When I came back, I took a lei of orchid and plumeria to Ed's grave, laid it on the green grass, and had a quiet moment of longing and love and remembering.

And here in Huntington Beach, I have seen azaleas, roses, and bird of paradise, growing in gardens and along the roads. Flowers serve the biological needs of the plants, of course, but there is no law that they have to be beautiful to do so. They could have been flat and gray just as well. Robinson Jeffers, a twentieth-century American poet who lived near Carmel most of his productive life, has captured that sense of miraculous joy in the poem he calls "Divinely Superfluous Beauty":

> The storm-dances of gulls, the barking game of seals,
> Over and under the ocean . . .
> Divinely superfluous beauty
> Rules the games, presides over destinies, makes trees grow

And hills tower, waves fall
The incredible beauty of joy . . .[1]

What teaches us gratitude better than diversity? In a world of apples, grapes, bananas, mangos, pineapples, plums, and papaya, where on earth did we ever get the idea as Mormon women that we should all look alike, sound alike, and talk alike? Just look at the Relief Society general presidency—one in purpose, one in desire to serve, one in love for the sisters of the Relief Society, but just about as different as you could imagine in terms of our backgrounds, our experience, our family situations, even our appearance. We don't all three understand the gospel in exactly the same way, and we don't all express our love the same way—but what's important is the gospel and that love. We can be diverse in other things as long as we are united in the important things.

Let me tell you a Japanese folktale about the importance of diversity—diversity in individual needs and diversity in meeting those needs.

Long ago and far away was a powerful lord who had the special hobby of collecting carvings of animals. When he was surveying his collection one day, he noticed that it lacked a mouse. So he summoned two of the skilled carvers of his kingdom to him, jingled a bag of gold before them, and announced his terms: "I want each of you to carve a mouse for me. Then I'll put them before my cat. Whichever mouse the cat pounces on first will go in my collection and its carver will receive this bag of gold."

So the two carvers, both feeling very motivated, went back to their homes and set to work. At the appointed time, they returned to the palace and presented their mice to the lord. One had carved a wonderful mouse out of wood with every hair, every whisker, in place. This was a dazzling mouse! But the other was nothing but a joke. The carver had used some soft material that flaked and would barely hold its shape. It didn't look like a mouse. It looked like a blob. And the carver wouldn't let the lord touch it.

The great lord was outraged. He could hardly believe that the carver was serious. "This wooden mouse is a marvelous piece of carving, but this thing wouldn't fool anyone, let alone a cat."

The carver, however, was unshaken. "Bring in the cat, according to the terms of the agreement," he said calmly. "The decision about which is the better mouse must be made by the cat."

The lord thought this was stupid but it *was* what he had told the carvers, so he ordered his servants to bring in the cat. No sooner was the cat on the floor, than it pounced upon the badly carved mouse, paying no attention at all to the beautifully carved one.

There was nothing for the lord to do but give the gold to the unskillful carver while the cat was worrying the other mouse into pieces, but as he did so he said: "Tell me how you did it."

"It was easy, my lord," said the man. "I didn't carve my mouse from wood. I carved it from dried fish."[2]

Sometimes do you feel like that cat, sitting around patiently hoping that someday somebody will carve a mouse out of something you can get your teeth into? We all have many different needs and wants. We all have many different skills and gifts. Our programs should reflect this diversity of gifts and needs. We should celebrate and cherish the diversity among sisters. And more than that, we should not wait for the Church programs to supply all of our needs. Maybe there's a sister in your ward who doesn't want a beautiful, lifelike mouse, no matter how carefully it is carved. Can you find a way to let her know that it's all right to pounce on the mouse that appeals to her?

Impermanence

The second point about flowers is that they are impermanent, lasting only a short time. This to me is a lesson in living in the moment, letting go of expectations about the future, and not trying to live in the past. Perhaps the ultimate expression of living in the moment is the beautiful counsel of the Savior to his Apostles when he was teaching them how to stop worrying about their personal needs and to rely with all their hearts upon the mercy and generosity of their Father in Heaven. He asked:

> And why take ye thought for raiment? Consider the lilies of the field, how they grow; they toil not, neither do they spin:
>
> And yet I say unto you, That even Solomon in all his glory was not arrayed like one of these.
>
> Wherefore, if God so clothe the grass of the field, which to day is, and to morrow is cast into the oven, shall he not much more clothe you, O ye of little faith? (Matthew 6:28–30.)

It's significant to me that the Savior repeated this same principle to the Prophet Joseph Smith and to the Apostles who were working to establish the restored Church a little over a century ago. There are only a few differences but they are significant ones. He told Joseph Smith:

> Consider the lilies of the field, how they grow, they toil not, neither do they spin; and the kingdoms of the world, in all their glory, are not arrayed like one of these.
>
> For your Father, who is in heaven, knoweth that you have need of all these things.
>
> Therefore, let the morrow take thought for the things of itself. (D&C 84:82–84.)

It is deeply comforting to realize that our Father, who is in heaven, knows what we need and promises to supply them out of his abundance and generosity; not merely grass but lilies, more gorgeously dressed than Solomon. How foolish we would be, then, to ignore the lilies and worry about a shortage of grass. The Father's love and providence is flooding us with his own joyous abundance of life.

Seasons

The third point about flowers is that they come in their appointed season, in the Lord's due time. When I left Salt Lake

City to go to Hawaii, the season of daffodils and lilacs was just ending. When I returned, the season of roses was just beginning. You know, there are many references in the scriptures to seasons. At least thirty-two times the scriptures refer to a "due season" or an "appointed season" or a "little season." This tells me that our Heavenly Father knows the seasons of our lives. He knows that there are seasons when it is right that something should happen, such as a season for being a student and concentrating on the joyous challenge of learning, or a season for concentrating on the responsibilities and blessings of motherhood. There are seasons appointed to us for intensive service, as on a mission or in a demanding Church calling. There are little seasons when we need the view of eternity to realize that a moment of tribulation—or maybe months that seem like millennia—will pass away if we can have the strength to endure it. Seasons come and seasons go.

I have found particular comfort in one scripture, a promise that the Lord made to the entire people of Israel but which I am applying to myself: "The Lord shall open unto thee his good treasure, the heaven to give the rain unto thy land *in his season*, and to bless all the work of thine hand" (Deuteronomy 28:12, italics added). Can we feel that openness to the Lord and the outpouring of his rain from heaven on our parched earth? What abundance and love we feel as he makes available to us his "good treasure," and how gentle is the promise that he will "bless all the work of thine hand" in his own season!

And I'd like to make another point, too. All of these meanings of "season"—due seasons, appointed seasons, and little seasons—are nouns. But "season" is also a verb. The Savior reminds us of this sense when he said, "Salt is good: but if the salt have lost his saltness, wherewith will ye season it? Have salt in yourselves, and have peace one with another." (Mark 9:50.) This is a time to see if we have salt in ourselves, if we are seasoned for the work. A crisis tests the strength that we already have. When the crisis comes upon us, it is too late to acquire the strength we need. Remember the story of the wise and foolish virgins? Let me quote it to you.

Then shall the kingdom of heaven be likened unto ten virgins, which took their lamps, and went forth to meet the bridegroom.

And five of them were wise, and five were foolish.

They that were foolish took their lamps, and took no oil with them:

But the wise took oil in their vessels with their lamps.

While the bridegroom tarried, they all slumbered and slept.

And at midnight there was a cry made, Behold, the bridegroom cometh; go ye out to meet him.

Then all those virgins arose, and trimmed their lamps.

And the foolish said unto the wise, Give us of your oil; for our lamps are gone out.

But the wise answered, saying, Not so; lest there be not enough for us and you: but go ye rather to them that sell, and buy for yourselves.

And while they went to buy, the bridegroom came; and they that were ready went in with him to the marriage: and the door was shut.

Afterward came also the other virgins, saying, Lord, Lord, open to us.

But he answered and said, Verily I say unto you, I know you not.

Watch therefore, for ye know neither the day nor the hour wherein the Son of man cometh. (Matthew 25:1–13.)

President Spencer W. Kimball had strong feelings about this parable and wrote a powerful and detailed interpretation that applies it directly to us as members of the Church:

I believe that the Ten Virgins represent the people of the Church of Jesus Christ and not the rank and file of the world. All of the virgins, wise and foolish, had accepted the invitation to the wedding supper; they had knowledge of the program and had been warned of the important day to come. They were not the gentiles or the heathens or the pagans, nor were they necessarily corrupt and reprobate, but they were knowing people who were foolishly unprepared for the vital happenings that were to affect their eternal lives.

They had the saving, exalting gospel, but it had not been

made the center of their lives. They knew the way but gave only a small measure of loyalty and devotion. I ask you: What value is a car without an engine, a cup without water, a table without food, a lamp without oil?

Rushing for their lamps to light their way through the blackness, half of them found them empty. They had cheated themselves. They were fools, these five unprepared virgins. Apparently, the bridegroom had tarried for reasons that were sufficient and good. Time had passed, and he had not come. They had heard of his coming for so long, so many times, that the statement seemingly became meaningless to them. Would he ever come? So long had it been since they began expecting him that they were rationalizing that he would never appear. Perhaps it was a myth.

Hundreds of thousands of us today are in this position. Confidence has been dulled and patience worn thin. It is so hard to wait and be prepared always. But we cannot allow ourselves to slumber. The Lord has given us this parable as a special warning.

At midnight, the vital cry was made, "Behold, the bridegroom cometh; go ye out to meet him." Then all the virgins arose and trimmed their lamps.

Even the foolish ones trimmed their lamps, but their oil was used up and they had none to refill the lamps. They hastened to make up for lost time. Now, too late, they were becoming conscious of the tragedy of unpreparedness. They had been taught. They had been warned all their lives.

At midnight! Precisely at the darkest hour, when least expected, the bridegroom came. When the world is full of tribulation and help is needed, but it seems the time must be past and hope is vain, then Christ will come. The midnights of life are the times when heaven comes to offer its joy for [our] weariness. But when the cry sounds, there is no time for preparation. The lamps then make patterns of joy on the hillside, and the procession moves on toward the house of banqueting, and those without lamps or oil are left in darkness. When they have belatedly sought to fulfill the requirements and finally reach the hall, the door is shut. In the daytime, wise and unwise seemed alike; midnight is the time of test and judgment—and of offered gladness. . . .

The foolish asked the others to share their oil, but spiritual preparedness cannot be shared in an instant. The wise had to go, else the bridegroom would have gone unwelcomed. They needed all their oil for themselves; they could not save the foolish. The responsibility was each for himself.

This was not selfishness or unkindness. The kind of oil that is needed to illuminate the way and light up the darkness is not shareable. How can one share obedience to the principle of tithing; a mind at peace from righteous living; an accumulation of knowledge? How can one share faith or testimony? How can one share attitudes or chastity, or the experience of a mission? How can one share temple privileges? Each must obtain that kind of oil for himself.

The foolish virgins were not averse to buying oil. They knew they should have oil. They merely procrastinated, not knowing when the bridegroom would come.

In the parable, oil can be purchased at the market. In our lives the oil of preparedness is accumulated drop by drop in righteous living. Attendance at sacrament meetings adds oil to our lamps, drop by drop over the years. Fasting, family prayer, home teaching, control of bodily appetites, preaching the gospel, studying the scriptures—each act of dedication and obedience is a drop added to our store. Deeds of kindness, payment of offerings and tithes, chaste thoughts and actions, marriage in the covenant for eternity—these, too, contribute importantly to the oil with which we can at midnight refuel our exhausted lamps. . . .

The day of the marriage feast approaches. The coming of the Lord is nigh. And there are many among us who are not ready for the great and glorious event.[3]

This message from President Kimball should cause all of us to search our hearts to see if we are ready for the events that will come upon us in the last days. But I apply his counsel in a way that is even more personal. When I think of the wise and foolish virgins, I take it as a very personal parable, one that tells me that my heart must be prepared at any moment and at all moments to receive the Savior's spirit, to hear his whisperings, to act upon his promptings. I do not always understand his timetable or sense the turning of his seasons. But I need to trust him and be ready. The season of flowers means that they do not exist for themselves but to produce fruit and seeds for the future. What are the fruits of the gospel? Paul said, "The fruit of the

Spirit is love, joy, peace, longsuffering, gentleness, goodness, faith, meekness, [and] temperance" (Galatians 5:22–23).

To me this scripture points toward the kind of lives we should live, the kind of saintliness that we should acquire, the kind of closeness we should have to the Savior.

In the season of sorrow that has come to me since the death of my husband, I cling to the scriptures. I cling to the promises of the Lord. I know that my own strength is not adequate to the burdens that are laid upon it now, but I also know—because I feel it every day—the strength of the Savior upholding me. I feel more than consoled. I feel uplifted and even propelled forward into the next steps that I must take. I find myself turning to the scriptures with an increased understanding of those prophets who suffered so much and yet who rejoiced in the Lord with an almost fierce exaltation in his glory and his might. Let me quote to you a passage from Isaiah that captures this feeling of jubilance, even in the midst of oppression. It even has something to say about flowers! "All flesh is grass, and all the goodliness thereof is as the flower of the field: The grass withereth, the flower fadeth: because the spirit of the Lord bloweth upon it: surely the people is grass" (Isaiah 40:6–7).

I know what this means. I saw my strong, vital husband collapsed on the sidewalk looking so fragile and powerless, then lying so helpless in the hospital bed. Mortality indeed means limitation. I feel that limitation and weakness in myself. But Isaiah continues:

> The grass withereth, the flower fadeth: but the word of our God shall stand for ever.
>
> O Zion, that bringest good tidings, get thee up into the high mountain; O Jerusalem, that bringest good tidings, lift up thy voice with strength; lift it up, be not afraid; say unto the cities of Judah, Behold your God!
>
> Behold, the Lord God will come with strong hand, and his arm shall rule for him: behold, his reward is with him, and his work before him.
>
> He shall feed his flock like a shepherd: he shall gather the lambs with his arm, and carry them in his bosom, and shall gently lead those that are with young. (Isaiah 40:8–11.)

Our Heavenly Father deals tenderly with us, caring for us gently. But his gentleness is not weakness. He is mighty! Isaiah continues by asking rhetorical questions that are almost a chant:

> Who hath measured the waters in the hollow of his hand, and meted out heaven with the span, and comprehended the dust of the earth in a measure, and weighed the mountains in scales, and the hills in a balance? . . .
>
> Hast thou not known? hast thou not heard, that the everlasting God, the Lord, the Creator of the ends of the earth, fainteth not, neither is weary? there is no searching of his understanding.
>
> He giveth power to the faint; and to them that have no might he increaseth strength. . . .
>
> But they that wait upon the Lord shall renew their strength; they shall mount up with wings as eagles; they shall run, and not be weary; and they shall walk, and not faint. (Isaiah 40:12, 28–29, 31.)

Isn't that glorious? If you feel that you are faint and faltering, remember that your strength is in the Lord, who can lift you on the wings of eagles! Sometimes our experiences with the Spirit are sweet and bright, like flowers; but their real purpose is to produce fruit—the fruit of a bone-deep knowledge of the Lord Jesus Christ, an unshakeable testimony that he lives and loves us and is our Savior. The gospel brings us many joyous moments, but it does not exist only for those moments in the present. Rather, it predicts—like an apple blossom in the spring— the sweet, solid fruit that will satisfy hunger all during the winter. Let us bring forth gospel fruits.

Conclusion

Truly the earth around us smiles in flowers, radiating the joy and love of our beloved Father in Heaven. And there are flowers in our own lives that bring joy, even though they may cling precariously to cracks in the rocks and even though fierce storms beat them down. Let's remember the four things that flowers teach us. First, one of the beauties of flowers is their diversity. Let's celebrate and cherish that diversity in our own lives, in our own children, in our own sisterhood. Let's not try to make people the same but use and honor the gifts we all have. Remember, there's a place for the well-carved wooden mouse and a place for the misshapen mouse carved out of dried fish!

Second, flowers by their nature are impermanent. They last only a short time. Let's remember that, and find joy in the present moment, not being burdened by the past or feeling anxious about the future. When things start to get you down, remember Okazaki chapter one, verse one and lighten up!

Third, flowers come in their appointed season, in the Lord's due time. If this is a difficult season for you, remember that it will pass and that you can, with the Lord's help, bear it.

Fourth, flowers are not meant to last. They do not exist for themselves but to produce fruit and seeds for the future. For us, the fruits of the gospel are love, joy, peace, and goodness. We trust in the power of the Lord. We have a Savior who understands our limitations, our loneliness, and our longings. He is with us always and has promised us that he will be with us forever. This is a promise we can trust. "The Lord shall open unto thee his good treasure, the heaven to give the rain unto thy land *in his season,* and to bless all the work of thine hand" (Deuteronomy 28:12, italics added). May it be so for us!

Notes

1. Robinson Jeffers, "Divinely Superfluous Beauty," in *Modern American Poetry/Modern British Poetry,* edited by Louis Untermeyer, (New York: Harcourt, Brace & World, Inc., 1958), p. 369.

2. "How to Fool a Cat," *Japanese Children's Stories,* edited by Florence Sakade (Rutland, Vermont/Tokyo, Japan: Charles E. Tuttle Company, 1958), pp. 74–76.

3. Spencer W. Kimball, *Faith Precedes the Miracle* (Salt Lake City: Deseret Book Company, 1977), pp. 253–57.

PART FOUR

Christ and
the Cause

11

Chosen for a Great Cause

*D*uring two crucial events of Christ's last days—upon his triumphal entry into Jerusalem and before Pilate—Jesus talked about his mission in terms of a cause. The first event was as the people of Jerusalem ecstatically greeted Christ on his entry into Jerusalem, and as the realization of his atoning sacrifice became more apparent Jesus uttered a prayer for strength: "Now is my soul troubled; and what shall I say? Father, save me from this hour: but *for this cause* came I unto this hour. Father, glorify thy name." Then in prompt witness of the Father's love for and support of this divine son, so soon to be sacrificed, "came there a voice from heaven, saying, I have both glorified it, and will glorify it again." (John 12:27–28, italics added.) Here Christ identifies his cause as the work of the Atonement. Only a few hours later, facing Pilate's demand, "Art thou a king then?" Jesus responded with a more specific definition of his cause: "Thou sayest that I am a king. To this end was I born,

This address was originally presented at the Women's Conference, Henderson Nevada Stake, 10 October 1992.

and *for this cause* came I into the world, that I should bear witness unto the truth. Every one that is of the truth heareth my voice." I've always thought it is sad and ironic that Pilate promptly disqualified himself from the group of those "of the truth" by asking, "What is truth?" (John 18:37–38, italics added.)

What is this truth of which Christ testifies? What is the cause for which he was born and for which he came into the world? I suppose there are different ways of answering that question, depending on which principle of the gospel we are emphasizing, but to me that great truth and that great cause lie in Jesus' answer to the lawyer who was trying to trap him about the nature of the most important law:

> Jesus said unto him, Thou shalt love the Lord thy God with all thy heart, and with all thy soul, and with all thy mind.
>
> This is the first and great commandment.
>
> And the second is like unto it, Thou shalt love thy neighbor as thyself.
>
> On these two commandments hang all the law and the prophets. (Matthew 22:37–40.)

To me, the cause of Christ is this dual commitment to love of God and love of our neighbors. On two very important occasions, we have also chosen the cause of Christ. In the premortal existence we chose God's plan which Christ supported over the plan of the adversary, signifying that our love for Heavenly Father and Jesus and our faith in a plan that preserved our agency to choose was stronger than our apprehension about mortality. And second, by joining the Church and taking upon us the name of Christ we have taken upon us the cause of Christ as well. What is this cause? Jesus has phrased it in terms of two commandments—to love God and to love our fellow human beings. Let me phrase those concepts in the very simple terms that make sense to me.

Christ was born, he lived, and he died to teach us how to love one another and to love our Heavenly Father. The gospel that he taught was one of love. The cause of Christ is to increase the amount of love in the world today—the amount of love in our hearts, the amount of love in our homes, the amount of love in our offices and businesses, the amount of love in our communities, the amount of love in our chapels, the amount of love in our nation, and the amount of love on our planet.

When we make room in our hearts for Christ and his abundant love for us, we are fulfilling the cause of Christ. When we think, speak, and act with love, we are carrying forward the cause of Christ. This is a great cause. It is the greatest cause we will ever know. It is the cause that prompted us in the preexistence to declare our allegiance to Christ, to trust him, and to desire to be like him so intensely that we were willing to take the frightening risks of mortality. We assumed the burden of freedom because we loved Christ so much. And he assumed the burden of being our Savior because he loved *us* so much.

Before we were born, then, we had become part of a web of love, like a cat's cradle, that sustains and supports us. It connects us with every other spirit and intelligence in the universe. It connects us with God himself and makes the atonement of Jesus Christ operational on our behalf if we will acknowledge the pattern and open our hearts to his love.

The cause of Christ is the cause of love. This is the work which we have chosen in these latter days and the work to which the prophets call us.

President Ezra Taft Benson said: "There has never been more expected of the faithful in such a short period of time than there is of us. . . . The final outcome is certain—the forces of righteousness will finally win. What remains to be seen is *where* each of us personally, now and in the future, will stand."[1]

Elder Jack Goaslind reminds us: "[You are] the valiant ones who must now step forward and carry out the assignments you committed to in your premortal life."[2] Elder Dean L. Larsen spoke these thrilling words:

> You have come to the earth when the foundation has been laid for this great work. The gospel has been restored for the last time. The Church has been established in almost every part of the

world. The stage is set for the final dramatic scenes to be enacted. You will be the principal players. You are among the last laborers in the vineyard. . . .

. . . We must keep the trust he has given us. We must qualify for his blessing by the way we remain different from the world in our obedience to his laws. Otherwise, we have no promise, and our fate will be the fate of the world.

. . . Remember the purpose for which you have come to the earth—the service you have been chosen to give. Stay true to the divine trust that our Heavenly Father and his Son, Jesus Christ, have placed upon you.[3]

My dear sisters and brothers, this is our cause, the cause of Jesus Christ, the cause for which we are chosen. We are to increase the amount of love in the world.

Now, let me share with you three thoughts I have about how to increase that love. First, let's make Jesus Christ the center of our lives. Second, let's make kindness a reflex. And third, let's find the joy in service that transcends projects to become personal.

Let Jesus Become the Center of Our Lives

First, then, let's make Jesus the center of our lives. Let the consciousness of Jesus Christ permeate our thinking until we live in a Christ-centered world. I love to think about Jesus. I love to sing hymns and Christmas carols, no matter what time of year it is. I love to repeat scriptures about Jesus to myself. Since Ed's death, the promise of the sacrament prayer has become so real to me. I am joyful when I promise that I will take the Savior's name upon me, and I am so grateful that he promises in return that I may always have his Spirit to be with me. I need that companionship. It's because I feel that companionship that sometimes I can get up, get ready, and walk out of the house. There have been mornings when I've stood with my hand on the doorknob and said right out loud, "Are you coming with me, Jesus?" I'll tell you the truth: there have been some mornings when I wasn't sure I could turn that knob and walk to my car. I needed so desperately to feel that companionship. But it's always been there. Feast on the scriptures. Keep a prayer in your heart. A prayer is really just like a conversation. I pray while I'm driving, while I'm riding in elevators, while I'm pushing a grocery cart.

To love the Savior with all of our heart, might, mind, and strength doesn't mean that we never think about anything else, never love anyone else, never work at anything else. It means that we think about other things in the presence of the Spirit of Christ. It means that we love others with the same kind of love that he gives us. It means that we work at our daily professions and assignments and Church callings and household chores and offer our good work to the Savior. And making him the center of our hearts enlarges our hearts in wonderful ways. You'll be amazed at how much room there is for other people, for kind words, for swift acts of service, for happy thoughts and gestures when your heart is filled with the love of Jesus.

Make Kindness a Reflex

Second, make kindness a reflex. As a schoolteacher, I became so keenly aware of how easy it was to misunderstand a child and hurt his or her feelings. I worked very hard to put myself in a child's place, to see what might be confusing or frightening, to see what might be reassuring or consoling, to learn what to say so that the child would have confidence to go forward and try. I don't think women are necessarily more gifted at sensitivity than men, but I think we're motivated to try harder, perhaps, because we're closer to children and see what happens when someone lets them down. I always love it at football games when the television camera zooms down for a close-up on these big rough, tough football players. And the first thing they always say is "Hi, Mom!" Doesn't that communicate a lot of faith? They know their mothers are watching. And would their mothers ever willingly let them down? I don't think so.

I remember when Kenny, our oldest son, was in first grade. I was teaching half days at two different schools, so I had time to come home and fix lunch for him even though we had to move fast. I used to look out the window when it was time for him to come down the street. He had the kindest heart in the world; and if someone didn't have a lunch, he would always bring that child home with him. And sometimes there were more than one! I'd count heads quickly and make a few more sandwiches or open another can of soup. Kenny was always amazed that I always had the right number of places set on the table and enough food for all. And I was always amazed that his heart was big enough for everyone who needed help. The best part for me was that my son knew I'd be willing to help and share.

There are so many ways of being kind. I think some of the most important are to include others, to give people the benefit of the doubt, to speak a kind word instead of a sharp word, never to make a joke at someone else's expense, not to judge others, and not to rub someone's face in a mistake. Let me tell you some stories.

It always hurts and grieves me when members of the Church condemn people who don't keep the Word of Wisdom and make them feel that they'll be welcome at church just as soon as they do. Ed and I would always say, "But these are the very people who should be in church most!"

Ed knew the problem from his personal experience. He used to smoke and drink when he was in college, but between the time we met and the time we became engaged, he quit. It wasn't as difficult for him as it is for people who have smoked for many, many years; but still, he had smoked while he was in the army. He had great empathy with people who were fighting this struggle every day.

And he also had great empathy with people who are stigmatized and punished because they can't win that battle immediately. Once he was attending a conference in San Francisco and, as was his custom, had looked up the address and meeting schedule of the closest ward. From the address he didn't know exactly where the chapel was, so early on Sunday morning he asked the desk clerk at his hotel where he could find the LDS chapel at such-and-such an address. A tall man who was also standing at the desk said, "I know where it is, and I'm driving right by there. I'll take you."

Ed thanked this stranger and got in the car with him. As soon as they pulled out onto the street, the man lit up a big, very black, very pungent cigar. Ed thought, "Oh, boy. Here we go!" But he would never have dreamed of saying a word to this man who was generously offering him, a stranger, a deed of kindness.

It was the longest ten-minute ride he'd ever had. When they got to the meetinghouse, the man said, "Here you go; have a nice day!" and zoomed off. Ed, reeking of very fresh cigar smoke, walked into the foyer. He had arrived just a few minutes before the meeting was to begin, so he approached a man standing alone, introduced himself, and said, "I'm a stranger in town. Where could I find the high priests quorum?" The man looked at Ed, sniffed, then literally looked away from him. Ed waited for a moment, then without saying anything else walked away. He knew from the layout of the building approximately where to find the classrooms, and could guess pretty closely from the ages of the men where the elders quorum was and which group was the high priests. He slipped quietly into the room and sat down on the back row.

As the aroma drifted over the room, heads turned all the way from the front, but then turned right back around again. No one greeted him. No one sat by him. No one asked him a question, asked him to introduce himself, or said hello. No one even looked at him. They communicated in every way they could, short of shoving him out the door, that he was not welcome there.

When I think about this experience, I feel just a little angry on Ed's behalf—that he should be treated like that—but he himself never felt angry. He was there to take the sacrament and renew his covenants and to learn more about the Lord, not to be intimidated by people who hadn't learned to have charity in their hearts for others. He was where he was supposed to be.

He knew it. He felt sorry for those people who were judging him.

I think, however, this experience changed his behavior. Often when we'd come into meetings he'd lift his head and inhale carefully. Then he'd squeeze my arm and say, "Let's sit over here," and I'd know that he had literally sniffed out someone who might feel like a stranger. He would walk up to someone who was standing there alone with that aroma surrounding him like a halo, smile, put out his hand, greet him, and have him talking and feeling comfortable by the time the prelude music was half over.

I think that Ed was like Mother Teresa: he saw the face of Christ in every human face. He never treated his boss differently from the way he treated the janitor. He always behaved with the same cordiality toward the bishop and toward the fourteen-year-old Scout. Remember what Paul said about love: "Charity suffereth long, and *is kind*" (1 Corinthians 13:4, italics added).

On another occasion, Ed was traveling for the federal government outside Utah and found the local ward for sacrament meeting. When he walked in the foyer, a Spanish-American man promptly came up to him, shook hands, and said, "Hello, brother! Are you new here? Do you need a place to stay tonight?" Ed felt truly welcomed, but he couldn't help noticing that a lady standing near them was looking at both of them coldly. He paid no attention to her and enjoyed the meeting.

His business meetings were with the representatives of a local Indian tribe, and that night the chief came to pick him up for the meeting. They were a little early, and the chief said: "I know you're Mormon. I'm not, but my daughter is, and I want you to meet our mission president." He drove up above the town to a beautiful neighborhood and pulled into the driveway of a large home. They got out of the car and rang the doorbell. The door was opened by the same woman who had seemed so uneasy and cold about Ed and the Spanish-American brother earlier that morning in sacrament meeting. She obviously recognized both the chief and Ed, and was very taken aback to see him, especially when the chief said, "Sister So-and-so, I know you want to meet Brother Okazaki here, because you have something in common. He's been a mission president, just like your husband." This sister was very embarrassed.

Now, another person might have felt tempted to make just the smallest remark to reinforce to this sister that she had made a mistake earlier that day, but not Ed. He smiled, shook hands, accepted her hospitality, sat down, and had a cordial conversation for the few minutes they were there. Kindness was a reflex with him. He could never have found even the smallest particle of pleasure in hurting someone's feelings—even if they might have had it coming.

You know, love and kindness and closeness to the Savior are joyful, happy things. They're not burdens to add to our already heavy responsibilities. Sometimes love, service, and kindness just sound like duty, and duty can sound like drudgery pretty easily. Well, lighten up! Don't take on more than you can do, and give yourself credit for everything you do. I want you to remember the joy, too!

Service: Make It Personal

Now, we've talked about two ways to increase love in the world: to make Christ the center of our lives and to make kindness a reflex. The third way in which we can increase love in the world is through service. Relief Society sisters throughout the world have done amazing feats of service, especially in community outreach during the sesquicentennial year. Often, organizing and performing a "project" is an institutional activity, and the rewards are also institutional. Think about some of the projects that you've participated in recently. What are some of the rewards? Yes, you get to associate with wonderful sisters from the ward, and being able to spend that time together is rewarding itself. Yes, there's genuine satisfaction in looking at a clean house, at a pile of quilts to be taken to a battered women's shelter, at seventy-two-hour emergency kits for every family in the ward. Yes, there's a wonderful feeling involved in knowing that you've helped someone. And there's a good solid reinforcement of loyalty, knowing that you've responded to the call of your leaders and been involved in a church-sponsored group activity. I don't want to suggest that any of these rewards are not genuine or that any of these reasons are not worthy. They are. They truly are.

But it is possible to spend hundreds of hours and never once see the face of an individual who is helped by our efforts, even though the heart of service lies in face-to-face communication—eye to eye, hand to hand, and heart to heart. Sometimes we think, "Oh, I want to give my service anonymously. I'm not doing it for thanks." I understand that feeling. It is a worthy feeling. There are many times when it is the only appropriate feeling. Of course it's important to write out those fast offering checks and quietly hand them to the bishop. Of course it's important to respond to the requests of our ecclesiastical and our Relief Society leaders. But we lose something precious, vital, and irreplaceable if *all* of our service is anonymous, if *all* of it is organized by someone else, if *all* of it is done as a group.

If we let someone else make all the decisions about service, faceless service can also become spiritless service. Let's not forget that other dimension of service—which, for want of a better term, I call personal service. Sometimes it's totally unsponsored and spontaneous. Sometimes it happens when you sign up and show up. But it always happens because you serve a person, not a project. You respond to a human need, not to a schedule with blanks to be filled. You connect with an individual, not just with a task.

Remember that the Savior said, "Inasmuch as ye have done it unto one of the least of these . . . ye have done it unto me" (Matthew 25:40). I take that statement with an absolute and trusting literalness. It is essential to think of its implications. We are performing a service for the Savior in rendering service for those who are less fortunate. We are commanded to seek the face of the Lord. Where should we look for him? We should look for him in the faces of the poor, in the faces of helpless children, in the faces of discouragement and bewilderment, in the faces of the hungry, the naked, and the homeless. And what is our reward? The Lord told Jeremiah, "Ye shall . . . find me, when ye shall search for me with all your heart" (Jeremiah 29:13).

Mother Teresa, who succors the dying and rescues babies abandoned on trash heaps in Calcutta, says, "We can do no great things—only small things with great love."4 She tends the dying and gives life to babies whose mothers threw them away, because she sees in each face the face of Christ. That's the real reason for doing service, to see the divine image in another human being and feel not only the bond of our own humanness but also the love of our Savior—love for us, love for that other person—enfolding and transforming and empowering us.

I recently returned from Huntington Beach Stake where I learned about a significant long-term project that the sisters of Huntington Beach Fourth Ward have taken on. Paul Pastizzo is a twenty-five-year-old nonmember who had been injured in an accident and left paralyzed from the neck down. Now, this is an organized project, right? It has a coordinator and a schedule and very detailed tasks that have to be performed. They're focused on some very specific outcomes. But this service is anything but anonymous and impersonal.

The Relief Society prepared a little booklet of letters written by women and their teenage children who had participated in this project. One of the things they stressed over and over again was their reawakened appreciation for their own blessings and their sense of connectedness with this individual they were serving. Trudy Witham wrote, "My adversities . . . seemed very small. I learned to appreciate the small pleasures of life, like eating Thanksgiving dinner with the family, when [Paul is] fed through a tube. To take a walk in the park with my husband when [Paul is] confined to those four walls the majority of time. To be able to talk and have people understand me while Paul has to repeat it frequently."

Gaye Zezulka said, "My family has received a feeling of giving and feeling good as to serving Paul." Jaunice Bair wrote, "I feel good about myself after I leave." Fourteen-year-old Adam Kent admits that he gave his mother "a hard time" when she made him help her with Paul's therapy. "But . . . after I went, I felt kind of good inside." Another fourteen-year-old, Tyler Moffett, said, "I hope many other young people can go and help Paul and feel as good as I did."

"Feeling good," they say. "Feeling good." I think speech therapists John and Claire Herbst put their finger precisely on the reason for those good feelings when they were serving Paul. They said: "We also felt the presence of the Holy Ghost with us."

Now obviously, part of the reason for these good feelings is because Paul is an exceptional young man, with a legendary smile, an inexhaustible fund of optimism and cheerfulness, and a warm appreciation of the services being given him. But I sense something else, too. Vicki Topliff describes, almost casually, a phenomenon that I think is pretty extraordinary. "When [Paul] really has something to say, we take the time to analyze each word. His voice is only a whisper, but with patience we can read his lips. When I have trouble with that, he says the words syllable by syllable. When even that doesn't work, he spells the words for me. It can take several minutes to express one thought, but it has become a kind of game for us. We both feel exhilarated when I finally understand what he is saying." Think of taking "several minutes" to decipher one thought. That's rather unusual in our busy world, isn't it? Why do you think it's so rewarding?

I want to suggest that it's because the Savior is there, sitting in the room with them, loving Paul, loving Vicki, leaning over Paul with Vicki, concentrating on each movement of Paul's lips, and guessing with her what the painfully articulated syllables must be. Another reason I have for feeling this way is something that Vicki reported her husband saying after he met Paul for the first time. Her husband said: "I'm connected now. Whatever pain he feels, I'm going to feel." This was during a time when Paul was hospitalized for double pneumonia and a bladder infection, but, says Vicki, "I have never seen Paul when he was unable to smile and joke." What makes the connections between people like that? Who else do we know who is connected with each one of us, who feels our pain, who has promised that he will never leave us nor forsake us? Those sisters in Huntington Beach Fourth Ward had a special reason to rejoice in their service, for they were feeling the presence of the Savior.[5]

Let me tell you another story. Sherri Zirker from the Mesa Arizona Twenty-second Ward described another very organized service project. Her Relief Society had an all-day quilting marathon—9:00 A.M. to 9:00 P.M.—with about 150 Relief Society sisters willingly donating supplies and labor. A newspaper article invited community members "to watch or participate in the quilting marathon." The purpose of the marathon was to supply some of the people in the Family Emergency Service Center in Mesa with bedding, and a very wise leader took the second step of bringing the quilters and the recipients in contact with each other. One of these women was named Martha. Sister Zirker writes:

> [Martha] had long been a recipient of others' "cast-off" goods, keenly aware she was given what somebody no longer wanted. To be the recipient of arduous effort in her behalf—having surveyed the cultural hall filled to capacity with quilting frames and busy women—created a desire within her, she later confided, to overcome all dependencies in her life by qualifying herself to someday be among those on the giving end.

She got to choose a quilt, and she selected a green one because it would remind her eight-year-old son of his favorite characters, the Teenage Mutant Ninja Turtles.

One nonmember visitor, awestruck, asked, "How do you inspire women to come out in such numbers?" This was wonderful, positive publicity for the Church. It was wonderful for the sisters to feel such a sense of achievement as they surveyed their accomplishments. But obviously the highlight was when families from the shelter came to select quilts to keep for themselves.

I think that often we are charitable and kind out of a duty

and a desire to serve, but we seldom see the people who are benefiting from the checks we slip into the fast offering envelope. Thus, to see human need looking out of the eyes of a homeless or a battered woman, to know that your quilt is going to provide warmth and comfort to a little boy who wishes he were as invincible and powerful as a Ninja turtle, is to see the human face of need. In such an environment, the result is love, mercy, and the Spirit of Christ. Sister Zirker suggests as much when she concludes, "The quilting marathon had the unexpected effect of creating ever-widening circles of charitable acts of love and concern, expanding the concept of sisterhood."[6]

You know, those sisters still could have drawn together in love over those quilting frames. They still could have gone home, tired and satisfied at the end of the day, with a solid sense of satisfaction at what they had accomplished. But I think there was a special glow, a special warmth inside most of them as they drifted off to sleep seeing Martha holding a green quilt for her son who liked Ninja turtles.

Sisters, the needs of the world are enormous. We can't do everything. We can't even do all of the good things there are to do. But please, set your priorities. Keep time for yourselves so that you can draw close to the Savior. Keep time for your families. Keep time for your sisters. And then find your own Marthas. Find a silence into which your voice can bring the note of sympathy and love. Find the loneliness that your smile can dispel. Find the need that your hand can fulfill. And find the human soul that yours can meet as a sister—not as faceless, anonymous charity.

Conclusion

We are engaged in the cause of Christ, to increase the love in the world. Let us do it by filling our minds with the thoughts of the Savior. Let us do it with kindness, by not judging, with joy and gladness of heart, by finding the connections that bond us rather than the distances that separate us, and by at least some service that is person to person, face to face, heart to heart.

As a united sisterhood, we can do miracles. But as single individuals, in partnership with the Savior, we can also do miracles; and not the least of these is what happens to us, ourselves, when we have that sense of working in partnership with the Savior, of knowing that he is beside us as we lean over a white, pain-drawn face, as we pick up a child who needs a snuggle, as we put a hot meal down before a hungry family. "Ye have done it unto me," he murmurs. "Unto me." And he has promised us our reward!

> Inasmuch as ye have received me, ye are in me and I in you. . . .
>
> And the day cometh that you shall hear my voice and see me, and know that I am.
>
> Watch, therefore, that ye may be ready. (D&C 50:43, 45–46.)

Let us watch for him. Let us watch for him in the eyes of the needy who are filled, in the sorrowing who are comforted, in the burdened who are relieved. I promise, we will find him there.

Notes

1. In "'You Are a Marked Generation,' President Benson Tells Students," *Ensign*, April 1987, p. 73.

2. In "President Benson, Youth Leaders Offer Counsel to 'Rising Generation,'" *Ensign*, July 1986, p. 72.

3. Dean L. Larsen, "A Royal Generation," *Ensign*, May 1983, pp. 33–35.

4. Dorothy S. Hunt, ed., *Love: A Fruit Always in Season, Daily Meditations by Mother Teresa* (San Francisco: Ignatius Press, 1987), p. 121.

5. [No compiler identified], "Thoughts on Working with Paul Pastizzo," photocopy of typescript (Huntington Beach: Huntington Beach Fourth Ward, [March–May 1992]), not paginated.

6. Sherri M. Zirker, "Circles of Love, Concern," *Church News*, 29 February 1992, p. 16.

12

"I Will Never Leave You"

$\mathcal{I}$ am so thankful every time I hear a prayer inviting the Spirit to be with us. I know that the Savior wants to be with us through the Holy Ghost. He listens to us. He yearns to bless us. If we are faithful, we can realize the fulfillment of the baptismal and sacramental promise that we will have the companionship of Jesus.

When I was a little girl growing up in my parents' home in Hawaii, we were Buddhists. There was a shrine in our home. We would make the offering or arrange the flowers, then we would bow and pray. Sometimes, I would go with my grandfather, a priest and a healer, high into the mountains near Kona, on the big island of Hawaii, where a Buddhist temple stood. We would chant the prayers together. Buddhism was my religious foundation. In it I learned about prayer, righteousness, service to others, honoring parents, and doing my best.

The original version of this address was given at numerous women's conferences in Japan and Korea during October 1992, with additional material from an address to the women of the deaf branches in the Ogden, Utah, stakes, 29 August 1992.

Then I became a Mormon. When hands were laid upon my head and I received the gift of the Holy Ghost, something changed in my heart. I had never felt that Buddha knew me or cared about me, but now I knew through the Holy Ghost that Jesus was with me. I had help in my decisions, comfort in my sadness. Jesus was not a statue in a temple. He was a personal God. He was my Savior. He knew my name. He was concerned about me. As long as I was pure and faithful, he was with me in the Spirit, whether I was walking on the beach of Mahukona or the sidewalks of Honolulu. I felt the Spirit strongly when I went to church, but I did not leave the Spirit behind me when I went home. It came with me.

The Reality of Jesus

How does Jesus become real and personal, a friend, a companion? I love the scripture: "Set me as a seal upon thine heart, as a seal upon thine arm. . . . Many waters cannot quench love, neither can the floods drown it." (Song of Solomon 8:6–7.) I think this is how we should feel about the Savior. He should be a seal upon our hearts so that we truly know that many waters cannot quench his love for us.

Let me give you an example. My husband, Ed, was an American soldier during World War II in the 442nd Regiment. It was composed of Japanese-Americans from Hawaii who were determined to prove their loyalty to the United States. They fought in the European theater of the war; and as a result of their determination, this unit had the most casualties and also the most decorations of any group in the army. My husband received a severe wound, and was decorated for his heroism. It took him almost a year to recuperate; but he was lucky to survive when thousands of his friends were killed.

Ed was a Congregationalist; but when he went away to war, his Buddhist grandmother gave him an *omamori*, a folded rice paper that contained a Buddhist scripture in beautiful calligraphy. Ed carried it all during the war as a gift of love from his grandmother, and I know that her love strengthened him. After the war, he put it in his billfold along with a little piece cut from the ribbon of his military medal. Later, he added a small family photograph of us. He kept this three-part *omamori* for more than fifty years in a little plastic cover and he had it in his billfold when his heart stopped beating just a few hours after the Relief Society sesquicentennial broadcast. Now I have it.

Ed had forgotten what the inscription said, and we had never had it retranslated; but if Ed had chosen his own *omamori*, I think it would have been these words of the Savior's: "Inasmuch as ye have done it unto one of the least of these my brethren, ye have done it unto me" (Matthew 25:40). That's just the kind of man Ed was. Ed did not have faith in characters that were brushed on the rice paper. He had faith in the Savior, and that faith was reinforced by the love he felt for family and the love he felt for his country.

I do not have an *omamori*; but since I have become the guardian of Ed's, I thought what I would choose to inscribe on mine. I think it would be a line from "Abide with Me!": "O thou who changest not, abide with me!" It is a prayer, spoken to the Savior. And the scriptures contain his answer: "I will never leave thee, nor forsake thee" (Hebrews 13:5).

If you were to make an *omamori* for yourself, what would you inscribe on it? What keepsake would you put with it? What would make it a seal upon your heart? We can have that comfort.

Do not feel that you need to be at the chapel to be in the presence of the Savior. He is with us as we talk to our children, as we wash our dishes, as we hurry to the market, as we greet others at our place of work. He understands the things that hurt us and worry us. He is with us when we grieve, just as he is with us when we rejoice. He understands when burdens become too heavy and when we become discouraged and exhausted. He understands that there are seasons when we must rest from our labors, like the winters, and seasons when our lives seem vigorous and new, like the spring. Do not walk away from him. Let him come with you.

Adversity

I know the Savior will be our companion, even in the most trying times of adversity and strain. I have truly felt his love and strength sustaining me and my sons when Ed was dying. Enduring that time was the hardest thing we have ever done, but we could do it. We felt the strength of the promise in the sacrament prayer, for we truly felt "that [we] may always have his Spirit to be with [us]" (Moroni 4:3).

Sometimes our struggles can seem discouraging, even overwhelming. I have a parable that I want you to remember at such times, a parable that Jesus told the Prophet Joseph Smith in the latter days for us.

> [Prepare] a feast of fat things . . . for the poor; yea, a feast of fat things, . . . that the earth may know that the mouths of the prophets shall not fail;
>
> Yea, a supper of the house of the Lord, well prepared, unto which all nations shall be invited.
>
> First, the rich and the learned, the wise and the noble;
>
> And after that cometh the day of *my* power; then shall *the poor, the lame, and the blind, and the deaf,* come in unto the marriage of the Lamb, and partake of the supper of the Lord, prepared for the great day to come;
>
> Behold, I, the Lord, have spoken it. (D&C 58:8–12, italics added.)

We are the members of Christ's body. We are his hands to do good and his lips to speak kindness to others. There may be many times when we think that the rich and the learned or the wise and the noble are more important, more able to make a contribution than we. But in the day of Christ's power, then shall the Savior welcome "the poor, the lame, and the blind, and the deaf." I think we can hasten that day by bearing our adversity well, by doing the little acts of kindness and service that fall within our power, and by seeing, even in the darkness of the world around us, the light that is our Savior Jesus Christ.

I graduated from the University of Hawaii. There I had met

Ed, whose education had been interrupted by his military service in Europe and by a year's recuperation. The year after we
both graduated we were married, and the year after that Ed
joined the Church. We went to Utah, where Ed completed his
Master's of Social Work degree at the University of Utah and I
taught school.

We had each other and we had the gospel. And soon we
had our two sons. But in many ways it was a hard time for us.
My parents were accepting and understanding, even as I left the
religious tradition in which they had raised me. Ed was not so
fortunate. His mother was very upset when he joined the
Church and, for twenty years after we moved to Utah, would
not answer our letters. Fortunately, Ed's sister and brother assured us that she always read them and always looked at the
photographs of our sons, so we knew that other feelings were
growing, under the silence.

We faced the challenges of prejudice, as did many other
people of Japanese ancestry in the United States, so soon after
World War II. But we did not give up. We did not become dis-
heartened when some members of the Church were distant, because other members were warm and welcoming. And now the
gospel has made bridges that are strong and sturdy, reaching
into many nations.

Service

Because of the Savior's life and death, his love has power in
us; and it manifests itself through our desire to perform Christlike service. What do I mean by that? First, it means that we
should minister to individuals in love, rather than worry about
administering programs. When we are truly filled with the love
of the Savior, we are more concerned about people than about
programs. If we are focused on programs, sometimes we get frustrated and impatient because other people aren't doing their
jobs right. We get angry feelings about them in our hearts. We
scold them. We make rules for them to follow. Sometimes we

frighten them, and sometimes their behavior improves. But what has happened to us? Our hearts are filled with angry feelings instead of with love. Then we feel ashamed because we are not behaving the way Jesus did. I think one of the reasons why we all loved President Spencer W. Kimball so much is that he never acted like an important person. He did not scold people. He was always kind. Whoever he was with was the most important person in the world for him at that moment. And as a result, he had endless love to give.

Elder Yoshihiko Kikuchi tells a wonderful story which illustrates how completely President Kimball strove to follow the Savior's example. When Elder Kikuchi was a counselor in the Tokyo Stake presidency, President Kimball, who was then President of the Quorum of the Twelve, visited the stake and held a meeting in the stake president's office. Because they wanted to accord the highest respect and honor to the Lord's anointed one and because they knew President Kimball had recently had heart surgery, they reserved the most comfortable chair in the office for him. It was padded leather, with armrests so that he could relax. Gently the stake president urged him, saying, "Here, President Kimball, please, please. The chair here behind the desk is for you."

"Oh, no," said President Kimball. "I have not come here to sit in the seat of honor, President. That is for you, not me. I am your servant." He went to the corner of the office, picked up a metal folding chair, placed it beside the desk, and humbly seated himself. Then he said, "Let's begin this meeting. Please tell me how I may serve you."

Elder Kikuchi relates that they felt his sweet spirit and were awed by his lowly heart and great humility. President Kimball's spirit and the essence of that simple lesson spoke to their spirits. "We all just sat there crying," Elder Kikuchi said, and tears came to his eyes again as he told this story.[1] In a simple gesture, President Kimball taught the leaders of that stake the attributes of the Savior: that no one should exalt himself above another, and that in meekness of heart we may all serve each other.

Isn't that an unforgettable lesson? I hope we all learn it.

Leadership is an opportunity to serve. It does not mean we are more important or that others should serve us. It also means that we serve individuals, not groups or programs or projects. Remember when Jesus healed the blind man? The disciples looked at the blind man but focused on the theological problem of who had sinned, the man or his parents, to bring blindness upon him. Jesus looked at him and saw an individual in need.

Let me share with you another example about the power of serving the individual. During Expo '70 in Osaka, one of the most memorable events was the visit of Crown Prince Akihito, now the emperor, to the Mormon Pavilion. He could visit only a few pavilions in the exposition, but he chose to visit ours. We were thrilled that he was coming. Ed sent for an orchid lei from Hawaii and asked the secret servicemen if it would be possible to present that to him. They said, "Absolutely not." They didn't want anyone that close to him, you see. One of our friends was the councilwoman from Ashiya City and was also a friend of the crown prince's family. She told President Brockbank, "Don't worry. Just have your daughter hide the lei behind her back and, when I give the signal, she can step forward and put it on him."

So the crown prince came in with his entourage. He was such a dignified, courtly, and gracious person. He shook hands with all of us. To Ed, he said, "I understand that you were one of the members of the 442nd Regiment." (In other words, the crown prince knew that he was a member of a unit of Japanese-American soldiers.)

Ed was astounded, but he managed to answer, "Yes, I was."

The prince continued, "I heard that you were wounded during the war."

"Yes," said Ed, "I was."

"How is your wound now?" inquired the prince.

"It's healed," said Ed. "I'm really doing very well."

"Good," said the prince. "I'm certainly glad that you're doing so well."

I'm sure the secret service had done the research, checking on Ed, but it was such a thrill to us that the crown prince knew that little detail and inquired so graciously about Ed's welfare. It was especially touching because, at one point, they would have been enemies; and by making the inquiry, the crown prince reached across the old gulf of World War II to see, not an enemy, but an individual.

Then the councilwoman gave the signal, and Sister Brockbank's daughter stepped forward, lifting the lei to put it around his neck. The secret servicemen leaped forward to stop her, but the crown prince threw out his hands, ordering them back. He bent his head for the lei and adjusted it on his shoulders, shook hands with her, thanked her, and walked around the pavilion wearing the lei. He filled our hearts with happiness because he took a sincere interest in us—just a little handful of Mormons whom he saw only for a few minutes and whom he would probably never see again.

We learned a great lesson from the crown prince. The Apostle Paul wrote to the Thessalonians: "We beseech you . . . to know them which labour among you . . . and to esteem them very highly in love for their work's sake" (1 Thessalonians 5:12–13). Can we feel this way about the people in our wards? Do we know their names, including the names of the children? When we ask someone, "How are you?" can we listen sincerely to the answer? We do not need to judge as we listen. We do not need to take on their problems. We do not need to give them advice unless they ask for it and unless we feel inspired to give it. We do not need to carry their burdens away with us. It is not our job to fix their problems; but it is our job to be with them in a loving and sustaining way while they deal with their own problems. In this way, we bear one another's burdens.

There is a great strength in a loving union. When Ed and I left the mission, the members presented to us their own version of a *senninbari*, an embroidered belt made for a warrior by his village. It was a beautiful stitchery showing a bouquet of iris. They had sent it from branch to branch throughout the mission, and every adult member, even the men, and the older children had taken a stitch in it. It hangs in our bedroom, where Ed and I could see it every morning when we woke up. The colors and the design are beautiful. The craftsmanship is exquisite, but what lifted our hearts was the love we felt in every stitch. We truly felt united with the thousand hearts that had produced it. Now Ed is gone. But when I look at this iris *senninbari*, I feel the same lift of the heart. It is a gift of love—like the gift of the Holy Ghost, like Ed's *omamori*.

Japanese villages no longer make *senninbari* to strengthen their warriors with the might and support of the entire village. But in each ward and branch of the Church we are making invisible *senninbari*. Each word of love can be a stitch in a beautiful pattern. We add our part to this fabric of love when we tell our young people, "Be strong. Keep the faith. We trust you." We tell each other as sisters, whether married or single, "We understand your challenges. We cherish your differences. We love you." We tell the men, "We appreciate your strength. We are here to help you. We are your partners in righteousness." Truly, in a ward of love and support, each member should leave the services on Sunday feeling encouraged and strengthened for the next week, wearing an invisible *senninbari* that contains the hopes and prayers and trust of the entire ward.

The Importance of Little Things

Satan often tries to persuade us that we should not be involved in the business of miracles. Sometimes he tells us that we are not important enough to perform significant service. Next, if he fails to get us with that one, he tells us that we have no truly significant service to perform. Mother Teresa says, "When someone tells me that the sisters have not started any big work, that they are quietly doing small things, I say that even if they helped one person, that was enough. Jesus would have died for one person, for one sinner."

And maybe you think, yes, but Mother Teresa is doing an important work, there in the slums of Calcutta. She says it is worth doing for just one person, but her work is much more important because she is saving the lives of abandoned babies and bringing joy to the dying. I cannot do a work *that* important.

Who is to say what is important? I think that giving a five-year-old in California a peanut butter and jelly sandwich with a smile is as important as praying beside the bed of a dying man in Calcutta. Mother Teresa thinks so, too. She says: "What we are doing in the slums, maybe you cannot do. What you are doing in the level where you are called—in your family life, in your college life, in your work—we cannot do. But you and we together are doing something beautiful for God."

Isn't that a wonderful idea? The peanut butter sandwich in California and the dying man in Calcutta—both of them are something beautiful for God. I love Mother Teresa because she knows the power of little things. She says:

> The whole world: it sounds so big and so much!
>
> One at a time. That one is Jesus. Yes, it is Jesus, because he has said so, "I was hungry and you fed me."
>
> . . . What we do is nothing but a drop in the ocean.
>
> But if we didn't do it, the ocean would be one drop less.
>
> We have no reason to be despondent or discouraged or unhappy, because we are doing it to Jesus.
>
> I know that there are thousands and thousands of poor, but I think of only one at a time.
>
> Jesus was only one and I take Jesus at his word.
>
> He has said, "You did it to me. . . ."
>
> My sisters, the brothers, and I, we take one person, one individual person, at a time.
>
> You can save only one at a time. We can love only one at a time.[2]

I hope that all of you can find your one to love, your own to serve. Keep your spit and your fingers handy. You never know when the Lord will ask you for a miracle.

I recently read about an ordinary woman who accomplished extraordinary things because she did not think of herself as an unimportant person or of her service as unimportant either. Delpha Triptow of Salt Lake City adopted as her own project a complete inventory of the Salt Lake City Cemetery tombstones when she discovered that the last record had been made in

1905 by university students. With a little funding that lasted for two years, she started her project; and when the money ran out, she simply started recruiting and training volunteers, ultimately 227 of them. She said:

> We found wooden markers which the weather had worn almost to obliteration. . . . Markers were made of white and red sandstone, marble, granite, metal and glass. Some were just hunks of cement embedded with spent bullet shells to form the names and dates. . . . On some of the sandstone markers, we would rub powdered corn starch on the stone and fill in the crevices [so we could read them] . . . In some cases we had to use garden spades to dig down into the sod to read the letters where the sod had grown up over the information. On white sandstone sometimes we used wet grass to rub across the letters to make it readable. On others, we used a thin sheet of paper and a carpenter's crayon to make an imprint from the stone.

One young man adopted Delpha's project for his Eagle Scout project, enlisted his entire troop to help, and painstakingly reconstructed a marker that was just a mass of crumbled stone, until they could decipher its information. One volunteer was a Japanese Buddhist couple who helped translate stones with Japanese characters. All together, Delpha and her volunteers have helped preserve the names of 130,000 individuals. Was that an unimportant service?[3]

Let me tell you one more story about the importance of doing the little things that come your way. On July 24 I attended a banquet sponsored by the Days of '47 Committee at which some very interesting awards were presented. They were called the Quiet Service Awards, and they were given to people who had quietly and persistently performed a service. One of these awards went to Maxine Grimm, the mother of the Church in the Philippines. The first Relief Society meeting in the Philippines was held in 1945 in her home (she was there as a Red Cross volunteer), with three present. Now there are more than 79,000 Relief Society members in the Philippines's 44 stakes and 650 districts; and more than 7,000 Relief Society sisters participated in special meetings as part of regional conferences in Manila, Cuba, and Bacolod.[4] Did Maxine Grimm think, when she invited two women to join her for a Relief Society meeting, that she was doing a great thing for God? As Jesus said, "Out of small things proceedeth that which is great" (D&C 64:33).

Remember that wherever you reach out in service, wherever you serve "one of the least," you are doing it for Christ and to him. So never think that, because you may have a physical handicap or limited means, you must be exclusively a recipient of service. Remember that God does not measure the size of the deed, but the amount of love with which it is done.

Our Connection with Christ

We believe that as part of the body of Christ, as members of his church, we share in his power. It is not our own power that we need to rely on but his. President Ezra Taft Benson, speaking at the October 1985 general conference said: "The Lord works from the inside out. The world works from the outside in. The world would take people out of the slums. Christ takes the slums out of people, and then they take themselves out of the slums. The world would mold [people] by changing their environment. Christ changes [people], who then change their environment. The world would shape human behavior, but Christ can change human nature."[5]

My dear sisters, what is your testimony of Christ? What do you believe about him? What experiences in your life have shaped your response to him? During the painful days after Ed's death, I clung to the promise of the sacrament prayer—"that they may always have his Spirit to be with them." Those were lonely days for me. These days still are. But I never felt isolated or abandoned. I clung to that promise in the sacrament prayer, and I felt the Savior with me. I had to learn to walk without Ed, but I had the Savior's companionship and I still do.

I have thought about ways the Savior described himself: as the bread of life, giving us strength and power to do our work; as living water which, if we drink, will cause us never to thirst again; and as the light of the world. What does it mean that Jesus is the light of the world? How can that help us bear our adversity and understand how we should serve others? According to Stephen R. Dimmitt, who reflected on the same passage of scripture, the metaphor means several things. First, light is absolutely essential to our physical life, as Christ is absolutely essential to our spiritual life. Sunlight is a crucial element in the process of photosynthesis in plants; a side effect of that process produces the oxygen human beings and animals need for survival, while our by-product, carbon dioxide, is the essential element for plants. Surely there is an analogy because the absolute necessity of our physical bodies for light and the absolute necessity of our spirits for "light in the form of the Holy Spirit, truth, wisdom, and Jesus' death and resurrection are the basis for maintaining our spiritual beings (John 1:4–5)."

Stephen Dimmitt's second point was that "light shines on everyone." Just so, Jesus' gospel was universal—regardless of people's wealth, righteousness, or ethnic group. We need to be sensitive to the historical fact that "we were once the undesirable, the outcast, the refugee—whether as Gentiles in the early days of the Christian movement or as martyrs in the early days of the Restoration. Can we," asks Stephen Dimmitt, ". . . not bring the light of the gospel to all?"

When we think about adversity, we must remember that each human being has burdens to bear. No one is exempt. Each of us can lift the burden of another. Remember that Jesus said an act as simple as offering a cup of cold water is a service to him.

The third application of the metaphor is that "light helps us see. There is probably no more terrible psychological plight than to metaphorically adjust ourselves to a lack of light. We are challenged by Christ's light to ask God to give us eyes to see where and how we can fulfill the mission of Christ: 'The Spirit of the Lord is upon me, because he hath anointed me to preach the gospel to the poor; he hath sent me to heal the brokenhearted, to preach deliverance to the captives, and recovering of sight to the blind, to set at liberty them that are bruised' (Luke 4:18)."[6]

It all comes back to Christ, doesn't it? We can deal with adversity and be full members of the community of Christ because he gives us strength. We can do small things with great love, because with Jesus there is no distinction between important service and unimportant service. We can see light in a dark world because Jesus is the light of the world.

Conclusion

My dear sisters and brothers, I plead with you to make real the promise that is renewed in us each Sunday when we take the sacrament. Let us remember the Savior. Let us have his Spirit with us. Let us set him as a seal upon our hearts, whether we have a literal *omamori* or just a special thought in our hearts. Let us feel sheltered and comforted by the Savior's love during our times of adversity. Let our hearts be sensitive in the service of others. Let us be concerned with ministering to our brothers and sisters rather than only with administering programs and projects. And let us feel the power of the promise of the Apostle Paul:

> Who shall separate us from the love of Christ? shall tribulation, or distress, or persecution, or famine, or nakedness, or peril, or sword? . . .
>
> Nay, in all these things we are more than conquerors through him that loved us.
>
> For I am persuaded, that neither death, nor life, nor angels, nor principalities, nor powers, nor things present, nor things to come,
>
> Nor height, nor depth, nor any other creature, shall be able to separate us from the love of God, which is in Christ Jesus our Lord. (Romans 8:35–39.)

Notes

1. My thanks to Elder Kikuchi for providing me with a firsthand account of this story, which I originally heard from one of my missionaries. Yoshihiko Kikuchi, letter to Chieko N. Okazaki, 13 March 1992.

2. José Luis González-Balado and Janet N. Playfoot, *My Life for the Poor: Mother Teresa of Calcutta* (San Francisco: Harper & Row, Publishers, 1985), pp. 38, 41, 20.

3. R. Scott Lloyd, "She Knew It Had to Be Done," *Church News*, 4 April 1992, p. 6.

4. "Growth Noted at Centennial," *Church News*, 4 April 1992, p. 7.

5. "Born of God," *Ensign*, November 1985, p. 6.

6. Stephen R. Dimmit, "I Am the Light of the World," *Saints Herald*, August 1992, p. 20.

13

"They That Are Christ's"

*G*alatians contains a beautiful scripture about the fruits of the Spirit: "The fruit of the Spirit is love, joy, peace, longsuffering, gentleness, goodness, faith, meekness, temperance: against such there is no law. And they that are Christ's have crucified the flesh with the affections and lusts. If we live in the Spirit, let us also walk in the Spirit." (Galatians 5: 22–25.)

That phrase, "they that are Christ's," seems powerful and strong. In it I see three implications for us. First comes the matter of identity—how we see ourselves when we think of ourselves as Christ's; second, how seeing ourselves as Christ's enables us to withstand adversity; and third, how we turn outward toward others when we see ourselves as Christ's.

The original version of this address was delivered at the following women's conferences: at Kauai Stake, 18–19 April 1992; at Maui Stake, 20 April 1992; at Laie Stake, 26 April 1992; at Kona Stake, 28 April 1992; with additional material from a sacrament meeting address in Maui on 19 April 1993. I also used portions of this address in my general conference address, April 1993; that address was published as "Cat's Cradle of Kindness," *Ensign*, May 1993, pp. 84–85.

Our Identity

The first point we need to discuss involves our identity. According to the baptismal covenant that we renew each time we partake of the sacrament, we take the name of Christ upon us. We become Christians. We remember Christ. We represent Christ. We have his Spirit within us. We act in his name. Our individual identities are modified by the identity of Christ. We become his friend, and we know that he has always been our friend. We know him. When we speak to someone, we do it the way Jesus would have done it. When we walk through a garden, our eyes are alive to its beauty and we praise its creator. Our hearts are centered on Christ. In him, the scriptures tell us, we live and move and have our being. Because we accept the Atonement he performed on our behalf we understand what the Apostle Paul meant when he said:

> Know ye not that your body is the temple of the Holy Ghost which is in you, which ye have of God, and ye are not your own?
>
> For ye are bought with a price: therefore glorify God in your body, and in your spirit, which are God's. (1 Corinthians 6:19–20.)

When I read the scriptures, I get a sense of the limitless love the Savior and the Father have for us. The scriptures describe the Lord's people as treasure, jewels, and as friends to him (see D&C 101:3; D&C 84:63). What a sense of celebration there is in this utterance from the Savior to the Saints of the Prophet Joseph Smith's day:

> Verily, I say unto you that ye are chosen out of the world to declare my gopel with the sound of rejoicing, as with the voice of a trump.
>
> Lift up your hearts and be glad, for I am in your midst, and am your advocate with the Father; and it is his good will to give you the kingdom. (D&C 29:4–5.)

In Deuteronomy, Moses tells the people that the Lord "set his love upon you" and "chose you": "For thou art an holy people unto the Lord thy God: the Lord thy God hath chosen thee to be a special people unto himself, above all people that are upon the face of the earth" (Deuteronomy 7:6–9).

How does it make you feel to hear scriptures like these? It gives me a wonderful feeling. I tingle and feel warm inside, as though something is bigger inside than outside. I feel joy. I feel wonder. I feel humility. I feel rejoicing and worship. And most of all, I feel a desire to be more like Christ, to know him better, to follow him better. Is it the same for you? It gives me that feeling from the line of one of my favorite hymns: "I stand all amazed at the love Jesus offers me" (*Hymns*, no. 193). I feel to say with the Apostle Paul:

> Blessed be the God and Father of our Lord Jesus Christ, who hath blessed us with all spiritual blessings in heavenly places in Christ:
> According as he hath chosen us in him before the foundation of the world, that we should be holy and without blame before him in love. (Ephesians 1:3–4.)

Withstanding Adversity

The second point involves dealing with tough times. When we see ourselves as Christ's, how does that enable us to withstand adversity? Once again, the scriptures are our guide. In that same lovely passage from the Doctrine and Covenants where the Savior says, "They shall be mine in that day when I shall come to make up my jewels," he continues, "all those who will not endure chastening, but deny me, cannot be sanctified (D&C 101:3, 5). Sometimes we receive trials from the Lord to chasten us. But many more times it is simply our lives in mortality that chasten us and try us. I think that the challenge we must deal with is whether we can focus our energies on dealing with adversity or whether we get sidetracked into accusing God of picking on us.

I have thought many times how Ed's death contains many of the elements that were important to him in his life. He spent the morning at the Relief Society sesquicentennial broadcast with me, supporting me with his presence and with his joy in the event. He loved all of the intercultural material presented on video that showed the gospel working for good in the lives of women all around the world. He loved greeting participants on the program, in the choir, and friends in the Tabernacle that day. He enjoyed a lunch afterwards with the other members of the presidency and their spouses.

There is no question in my mind that it was his time to go. Dr. Joe Jack, a surgeon, was walking beside him when Ed's heart simply stopped beating. Church security personnel trained in CPR were beside him almost immediately, and the hospital was only minutes away. He had a priesthood blessing within minutes. Many General Authorities prayed with us and gave him blessings. Everything that could be done, both spiritually and physically, was done. There is not one event I can look at and say, "If only this had been different" or "if only that had been different." Ed's last act of kindness was to linger long enough for our sons to reach his bedside and, with me over the next six days, accept that heartbreaking reality.

At the funeral, there was a feeling of peace and love and even joy that made the sorrow sweet. Our missionaries sang some of the songs that he'd loved in Japanese, and a choir of our Polynesian friends sang "E Hawaii Nei" and "Aloha Oe" in love and farewell. Ed *was* Christ's. He had been Christ's all of his life—first as a Congregationalist and then as a Mormon. And now he was with the Savior, and the Spirit of the Savior was with us. We sorrowed greatly and still do, but we can bear it.

Adversity comes to all of us in different ways. It is part of mortality. It is not a punishment. It is not a test to see how well we will do, even though it does test us. If we are Christ's, we will know that he is with us in our adversity as well as in our joy.

Let me share another story with you, the story of Allen and Marian Bergin of Provo, Utah, where Allen is a psychologist at BYU. They had six children, then Marian gave birth to triplet sons. When the boys had just turned two, Daniel somehow made his way to a neighbor's swimming pool. They found him floating face down on the surface of the water and rushed him to the hospital. He survived, but with permanent brain damage, unable to move or talk freely. At the time the article was written he was sixteen years old, still crippled and limited both physically and mentally, while his brothers were healthy, active, and energetic. It was and still is an experience of wrenching pain. You can imagine how the family—parents, brothers, and sisters—have struggled to come to terms with Daniel's cruel handicap. But it is also a beautiful story. His mother tells of trying to teach a group of young women from the ward about identity and personal growth. She was trying to teach them that we all have intrinsic worth, because we are children of Heavenly Father—"that we are not our achievements or our accumulation of possessions." She writes:

> Quite spontaneously, I decided to use Daniel as an example. . . . Most of these young women [knew] Daniel, by sight or from interacting with him. I asked the young women if he had any worth: he can't walk; he can't talk; he will never achieve worldly success. They vigorously agreed that he is a valuable person. They love to be around him. He radiates love, caring, purity. His spirit shines forth as a blessing to others.
>
> I believe those who were there experienced a vivid affirmation of what is really of worth in this life.

This may not be the special achievement that parents dream of for an unborn child, but perhaps it is the most important lesson of all for us to learn, we who are Christ's. Sister Bergin continues with other lessons she has learned about adversity:

> Sometimes I find myself believing that others are not suffering as I am, or even that the wicked are happier than I am. This has ever been a human inclination. But it is relieving to let go of such beliefs. One father, faithful in his service to family and the Church, told me, "I think my pain was increased by the idea that lots of other families were succeeding very well and that ours wasn't. I wanted to hide our private realities. Since then I have

learned that virtually every family faces one or more major crises, and I have learned that many of those we think are outstanding examples are about as inadequate as the rest of us." Such realizations can release us from the defeating belief that we will never measure up and allow us to concentrate on the tasks at hand.

It would be easier to correct our distorted beliefs about suffering if our culture did not drum into us a success syndrome. We hear about and focus on others' successes and outward happiness, but we seldom hear about talking with close friends or seeking out trusted loved ones with whom to share pain. Why do we hesitate to share our pain? Do we build walls to protect our images rather than building bridges to reach out to one another? When will we become a community of believers living together to love and support each other? (See Galatians 5:22–26; Ephesians 4:21–32; Philippians 2:1–3.)

I wish we were more open and that we trusted and loved each other more. Then we could talk about our pain, understand it better, and move toward acceptance of whatever we are dealing with. Acceptance does not mean we give up. It means we accept where we are and start making changes, finding solutions—no longer paralyzed by guilt, denial, depression, or anger.[1]

I literally do not know what we would have done without the love and support of all of the people around us, who put their arms around me and Ken and Bob and said, "We loved him too. He was such a good man. We will miss him." We can share each other's pain during adversity. And in so doing, we can serve as those who are Christ's should be able to serve others.

Serving Others

This brings us to our third point. When we are Christ's, we know that we are infinitely precious—jewels, chosen, special, and treasures—bought with an immense price. In fact, purchased with the life of the Son of God. Because Christ thought we were worthy of his life, we sense our infinite worth in the sight of God. I think this testimony not only enables us to bear our own adversity bravely but also enables us to reach out to others with love and support in Christlike service.

There's a Japanese word that captures this feeling: *kigatsuku*.
It means an inner spirit to act without being told what to do, a
willingness to serve, a self-motivated impulse toward goodness.
It involves seeing a need and doing what you can right then to
relieve the need.

Ed was the most *kigatsuku* person I've ever known. Let me
tell you just one example. When we moved back to Salt Lake
City in 1988, we moved into a neighborhood where some
people had lived for fifteen or twenty years. We didn't wait to
learn a few names each week at church or to recognize people
on the street as cars passed. We went visiting. Ed gave everybody little packages of fortune cookies. And we knew all of our
neighbors within just a few days. The bishop says, "You were
never new in this ward. You belonged, even more than some of
the older residents, from the first week you were here."

After the funeral, one of our neighbors on the street behind
us reminded me that the first winter we were there Ed had gone
throughout the neighborhood, house to house, saying, "The city
street department people have worked so hard to clean the
snow off the streets. We should let them know we appreciate
it." So he collected a few dollars from each neighbor. Then we
bought boxes of oranges and apples and doughnuts and drove
down to the Street Department and gave them to the workers.
They were so astonished they almost fell over. They said,
"Everybody complains if the streets aren't clean, but nobody has
ever said 'Thank you' before." My neighbor reminded me that
Ed had kept on doing that, quietly, every winter. "And my street
has never been cleaner after a snowstorm," she said, "than since
Ed started doing this for our whole neighborhood."

We in the general presidency have felt the *kigatsuku* spirit of
the whole Relief Society increase as a result of the community
service the LDS sisters gave around the world. Some New York
women wrapped packages at a mall during their own busy
Christmas season and earned the money for quilts which they
made for women and children in a shelter. Another group of
sisters in Hartford, Connecticut, takes the children from an or-
phanage in their area to McDonald's to celebrate birthdays. The
sisters of Riverton Second Ward in Utah provide service and

friendship to a home for mentally handicapped women. The women of Gugelethu Branch in Cape Town take in unsupervised street children. A group of Australian sisters are volunteers in a telephone service of contacting the handicapped, the housebound, and the aged.

Another place where the spirit of *kigatsuku* is strong is in missionary service. I'd like to pay special tribute to my own missionary, Sister Rosetta Colclough. She came to our elementary school when I was eleven and explained to each class that met in the library during study-hall period that a special class in religion would be taught at the little Mormon chapel near the school. Three other girls and I were curious, so we accepted the invitation and went to the Mormon chapel on our next study hall. That was the beginning of my religious instruction, and eventually, four years later, I joined the Church.

When Ed was dying, I received a letter from Rosetta Colclough Stark. She had been a teacher for many years in the Granite School District in Salt Lake City, then moved to Mesa, Arizona, after her husband retired. On the afternoon of the sesquicentennial broadcast, Rosetta Colclough Stark sat down at her typewriter in Mesa, Arizona, and wrote me a letter: She said:

> I heard your name announced by Sister Jack. . . . I sat up straight and watched the T.V. screen eagerly and saw your name appear on the screen. Then you started to speak. The dark hair has turned to silver, but that sweet face was easily recognized. Yes, this is my little Chieko whom I taught at the Honomakau Chapel in Kohala so many years ago. As I listened to your voice, tears of joy ran down my cheeks. . . .
>
> I thank my Heavenly Father that I had the privilege of teaching you about Jesus Christ our Savior in that little chapel at Honomakau in Kohala. I have been blessed three times because of it; first that I was there to experience that light from Heaven with you; second, that you came to my ward in Salt Lake City to speak, and today when I heard you speak to the women of the world via satellite.

While Rosetta Stark was writing that letter, Ed was being taken to the hospital, but her letter reached me with a special love on Wednesday or Thursday when we were dealing with the knowledge that Ed would not recover. She enclosed in it a little article she had written for her ward newsletter in 1978, fourteen years ago. I want to share it with you—not because it's about me, but because of the testimony of service that it breathes. Here is what she says:

> Back in 1938, I was called on a mission to Hawaii. Because I had been a school teacher, my special calling was to open what was called Religious Education [in Kohala]. . . . Many of my students were Japanese. They were from homes where Buddha was the only religious leader they knew much about. I taught them stories from the Old Testament first, then later introduced them to Christ.
>
> One day on the eleven o'clock period, only four students came to class. I was very disappointed there were so few. They were four Japanese girls. Near the close of the period, we stood in the little chapel with bowed heads and closed eyes, repeating in unison, "The Lord's Prayer." The soft Hawaiian sun filtered through the windows. As we prayed, I suddenly felt a bright light envelop us, coming from above like an inverted cone. A wonderful feeling of peace and joy filled my heart. I led the prayer very slowly as the bright light enfolded us. I was sure the girls felt it also, as their faces shone with an expression of deep reverence. We almost whispered "Good-bye" so as not to break the spell, and they tiptoed out. I thought, "One or more of those girls will join the Church and become a great influence for good."
>
> At the end of the school year, our classes were over and I was transferred to another island. Two elders continued the classes the next year. My mission soon ended and I returned home. Often the sweet faces of those four girls passed before my inward eyes, and I wondered about them. There was one, Chieko Nishimura, that lingered in my mind, and I often looked at the picture I had taken of them.
>
> Ten years later, my husband and I were attending our sacrament meeting in the Imperial Ward, Salt Lake City, when it was

announced that a young Japanese couple from Hawaii would be the speakers. . . . My heart nearly jumped up into my throat. Yes, it was my little Chieko. . . . Chieko and I had a joyous reunion after the meeting. We marveled that out of all the many wards in that big city, they should have come to speak at my ward. We were sure the Lord had a hand in it.

As the years went by, I saw her picture several times in the *Church Section* of the *Deseret News* and articles telling of her outstanding accomplishments in positions of Church leadership.

I finally lost track of them. [Remember, she was writing this in 1978 when Ed and I were living and working in Colorado.] But I'm sure the light of their faith blessed many souls as they traveled onward through life. [Now, here's the message that Rosetta was trying to convey by telling this story.] Sometimes when we feel we are doing but little, we are in reality helping to accomplish the Lord's purposes, and He is guiding us. How far the beams from one little candle can travel! Each of us must let the light from our candle shine forth. We know not into what depths it may eventually penetrate.

I did not see the light she saw while we four little Buddhist girls repeated the Lord's Prayer, phrase by phrase, after this Mormon missionary. But I know the Spirit whispered to me during that experience, reminding me of my true identity as a daughter of God and prompting me to let those teachings sink deep into my heart so that I could also become a daughter of Christ in the waters of baptism. Rosetta Colclough Stark blessed me as a missionary, blessed me again when our paths crossed briefly in Salt Lake City, and blessed me a third time through her letter, reminding me of Heavenly Father's great love for me at a time when I was suffering such pain as Ed lay dying. I needed that reassurance and love. I needed to remember that Heavenly Father had reached down and laid his hand on a skinny little eleven-year-old Buddhist girl and said, "You are my jewel, my treasure, my chosen."

I've shared this story with you, not because it is about me, but because it shows two other points. The first is the point that Rosetta Colclough Stark makes—that we never know the effect of our service. Do you remember the message of the Primary song, "Shine On," in *Children's Songbook* (no. 144)?

> My light is but a little one,
> My light of faith and prayer.
> But lo, it glows like God's great sun,
> For it was lighted there.

All service counts. No service is small to God. We all have enough to share, however scanty our resources may seem to us. Sister Mary Ellen Edmunds, one of the sisters on the Relief Society General Board, was the first welfare services missionary in Indonesia in 1976. In the sesquicentennial issue of the *Ensign*, she paid a tribute to the Indonesian sisters she knew. "These Relief Society sisters, led by their president, Ibu Subowo, were giant souls in small bodies," she wrote. "Every morning before they began their cooking, each sister would hold back a spoonful of rice. They kept the rice in plastic bags that they brought to Relief Society each week. After the meeting, they would gather and prayerfully consider who needed a visit. All would then go together to visit those in need, taking the bags of rice with them to share with those who had less than they did."[2]

I'm sure that in every congregation there exists a wide range of resources and means. Some of you may feel that you have very little to share. Do you have a spoonful of rice? Remember, when Jesus healed the blind man, he only had a little spit and a little mud, but it was enough to make a miracle.

Christian service connects all of us in a network of love that is strong and beautiful. A piece of string is not very interesting, not very strong, not very beautiful, but with it and a little skill you can create the simple yet intricate pattern of a cat's cradle. I learned dozens of patterns as a child and can still make the pattern called two-eyes and even five-eyes. It is complex and beautiful. Each part supports the other parts and is connected to them. Every part is important. Every part is essential. No part is the "boss" and no part is the "subordinate." Rosetta Stark is part of this pattern. I am part of the pattern. Ed is part of the pattern.

You are part of this pattern. It is the Savior's pattern, and I sometimes like to think that the eyes looking out of this pattern are his eyes, watching us, his children.

President Gordon B. Hinckley said something that I just love about our interconnectedness. He wasn't talking about cat's cradles, but I think he could have been. He said:

> My co-workers in this great cause and kingdom, you and I are weaving the grand design of that standard to the nations. It waves to all the world. It says to men and women everywhere: "Come, walk with us and learn of the ways of the Lord. . . ."
>
> To those of the Church, all within the sound of my voice, I give the challenge that while you are performing the part to which you have been called, never lose sight of the whole majestic and wonderful picture of the purpose of this, the dispensation of the fulness of times. Weave beautifully your small thread in the grand tapestry, the pattern for which was laid out for us by the God of heaven. Hold high the standard under which we walk. Be diligent, be true, be virtuous, be faithful, that there may be no flaw in that banner.
>
> The vision of this kingdom is not a superficial dream in the night that fades with the sunrise. It is veritably the plan and work of God our Eternal Father. It has to do with all of His children.[3]

I thought about service a great deal while Ed was dying. You know how it is in a hospital. The minutes seem to drag by on leaden feet, even though the days and nights pass in a blur and you long to have them slow down so you can get your breath. I had a great deal of time to think and reflect. I noticed many things. And I learned a great deal about service.

One of the things I thought about is how we all want to be special. We all want to feel that we are special to someone, specially beloved and cherished. We want to be treasures and jewels and chosen to other people as well as to the Savior. Well, the way to do that is through service. I will never feel the same way again about the people who served Ed and me and our sons while we were in the hospital. I care about them in a new way. And because they have served us, I know that they care about us in a new way. Remember the cat's cradle—when we are woven together in service, we make a pattern of love. It is that *kigatsuku* feeling, and it has nothing to do with ward callings. It has to do with spontaneous kindness and Christian service.

Ed had that *kigatsuku* sense to overflowing. I received a touching letter from Hiroshi Shirota of Los Angeles after he heard about Ed's death. In it he said:

> I hardly knew Ed back in 1954 when I returned from an overseas job. Yet when I told him I wasn't feeling well, he took the trouble to have me admitted to the Veterans' Hospital in Salt Lake City for a month. He came to visit me whenever he could and made sure I received proper care. I was deeply moved. But then, Ed was that kind of a guy. He cared for everyone with that deep warmth and wonderful aloha in him. I feel privileged that I had known Ed. When I'm around guys from the 442nd, I always ask if they had known a friend of mine, Ed Okazaki. I was always proud that I could call him a friend. . . . He exemplified everything that was good in a man. A complete man. I hope someday someone can say as much for me, too.[4]

I was very touched by Hiroshi's phrase, "a complete man." A complete man. A man who was Christ's. Ed had perfected the ability to love the sinner without excusing the sin, to identify sin without judging and rejecting. He had something else, too, in his charity—an ability to combine personal charity and institutional charity. I know many good members of the Church who are generous with their means, who will willingly write out a check for a good cause, and whom the bishop can always count on if the mission fund or the welfare fund seems to drop a little. When our bishop, just two weeks before Ed died, gave an inspiring talk about the need for generous fast offerings, Ed came home, wrote out a check, and took it over to the bishop's before we sat down and ate dinner. Some people are good neighbors and kind to their friends and family, but they do not often step outside to render service to a stranger. There is sometimes a barrier in their minds that draws a line between people they are responsible for and people they aren't. This line did not exist for Ed.

It is not our job to decide whether someone deserves our help or not. Sometimes the bishop has to make decisions like that because the Church's funds are involved, but we are free from that burden and we can help—just as much or as little as we like, according to our desires, our abilities, and our needs. In Salt Lake City, a large group of homeless people, mostly men but also some women and children, gather under one of the viaducts on Sunday mornings, where a woman named Jeannie has been coming for eight years, serving the food that volunteers bring. Ed went down two Sunday mornings himself, in February, taking a case of oranges that he'd picked up on sale. It was so like Ed to just quietly show up in a place on the chance that he could be useful. I was out of town for conferences, but the third week I could go, too, and we went together. I was asked to number each paper plate so that the people waiting could be called up in order.

Jeannie said, "Write the numbers, and then under each number write, 'God Loves You.'" So I did.

As I looked at those men, most of them apparently able-bodied and not mentally retarded, I wondered why they were homeless, why they could not find a job or keep steady employment, and what paths in their lives had brought them there. But I felt strongly that I could not judge, that I had to meet them just where they were and just where we were that morning.

So I spoke to each one, smiled, and said, "Hello." So many of them seemed actually startled that I would speak to them that it hurt me a little bit. One of the young men—he seemed to speak with an accent and may have been from another country—picked up his plate and looked at the words, "God Loves You" written on it.

He started to walk away and then said to me, "God loves me." I said, "Yes."

He said, "Thank you that God loves me. I know God loves me."

When we had to leave, I saw him sitting down on the grass eating his breakfast. He saw me and waved. It was his smile I'll remember from that experience.

And when we went back the next week, there was the same man. He recognized us and greeted us. I sensed no feeling of judgment about him—only warmth for him. What if I had judged him? What if I had said to myself, "This man is not worthy of my help until he can convince me that he is ready to get a steady job?" I would have missed that wonderful warm feeling in my heart that I know was charity, or the pure love of Christ. And I would have missed sharing a sweet, sweet experience with my husband, who was, so soon, going to be taken from me.

I want to tell you one more story about not judging, about being willing to share what you have, and about the blessings that come from our willingness to serve. Bishop Clarke told this story in conference, but he was quoting a story that was in a priesthood manual lesson during the 1970s. The person who told this story was not identified, so I can't tell you who the speaker or the grandmother might be, but it is a lovely story of service and sacrifice:

> Many years ago in a small town in the southern part of the state of Utah, my great-grandmother was called to be the president of the Relief Society. During this period of our Church's history there existed a very bitter and antagonistic spirit between the Mormons and the Gentiles. In my great-grandmother's ward one of the young sisters married a Gentile boy. This of course did not please either the Mormons or the Gentiles very much. In the course of time this young couple gave birth to a child. Unfortunately the mother became so ill in the process of childbirth that she was unable to care for her baby. Upon learning of this woman's condition, great-grandmother immediately went to the homes of the sisters in the ward and asked them if they would take a turn going into the home of this young couple to care for the baby. One by one these women refused and so the responsibility fell completely upon her.
>
> She would arise early in the morning, walk what was a considerable distance to the home of this young couple where she would bathe and feed the baby, gather all that needed to be laundered and take it with her to her home. There she would launder it and then return with it the next day. Great-grandmother had

been doing this for some time when one morning she felt too weak and sick to go and perform the service that had become her custom. However, as she lay in bed she realized that if she didn't go the child would not be provided for. She mustered all her strength and went. After performing this service she, and I suppose only with the help of the Lord, was able to return to her home and upon entering her living room, collapsed into a large chair and immediately fell into a deep sleep. She said that as she slept, she felt as if she were consumed by a fire that would melt the very marrow of her bones. She began to dream and dreamed that she was bathing the Christ child and glorying in what a great privilege it would have been to have bathed the Son of God. Then the voice of the Lord spoke to her saying, "Inasmuch as ye have done it unto the least of these, ye have done it unto me."[5]

Obviously we all need to contribute money, for there is great strength in our ability to do good when our organized efforts join with those of other people. But something is missing from our spiritual lives if we never see a need ourselves and meet it. When we look into the eyes of someone whose suffering we are alleviating, when we touch their hands and speak to them ourselves—not through intermediaries—then we claim the great promise of the Savior with a power and a directness not available if there is distance: "Inasmuch as ye have done it unto one of the least of these my brethren [and sisters], ye have done it unto me" (Matthew 25:40). Ed knew this. This is how he behaved.

Bruce Haglund, one of our missionaries who flew up from California to Ed's funeral, called me a few days afterwards to see how I was doing. And then he said: "I thought you'd like to know about my trip home. I was sitting in my seat waiting for takeoff when this big woman came down the aisle—and I mean big, big, big! She was sitting next to me and just brimmed over. She could have easily used both our seats. I huddled as far as I could get against the other armrest and was feeling pretty resentful about being crowded. Then suddenly the thought occurred to me, 'What would President Okazaki do in these circumstances?' And I knew exactly what he would do. So I did the same. I smiled at the woman, introduced myself to her, and began talking to her. We had a fine conversation all the way back. I learned so much from her. I think she was the nicest person I ever met. My trip home was so pleasant. I felt so good about that experience and so grateful to be liberated from all those negative judgments. And so grateful to Ed for teaching me how to be."

My dear brothers and sisters, one of the greatest privileges and opportunities of mortality lies in our ability to serve others. I have thought a great deal about what life must be like in the next world, because I would like to know what Ed is doing. I know he is involved in service, but I wonder what kind? I think some forms of service are experiences that we can have only in mortality. No one is hungry in the next life; so if we want to share food with those who weep from hunger, we must do it in this life. No one is cold or naked. If we want to give a pair of shoes to a barefoot child, we must do it in this life. We know that the wicked suffer remorse, but there is no indication in the scriptures that there is grief or loneliness or sorrow among those in paradise. So if we want to give comfort and encouragement, we must do it in mortality.

This is our day. This is our chance. Let's take it! Our path through mortality may be long or short, straight or curved, smooth or rocky. But we have the power to make our path the Savior's path. We can be his hands to do good, his feet to run swiftly on errands of mercy, his love to heal and bless others.

Conclusion

My dear sisters and brothers, I testify to you that something remarkable happens when we see ourselves as Christ's. Our identity changes. We treasure ourselves more because we know how valuable we are, and we treasure others, because we know how valuable each individual is to Christ. Once we see ourselves in this way, we can withstand adversity and pain without becoming bitter and without turning away from God. We understand our suffering in a new way, and we continue to feel loved and cherished even in our pain. And we serve in new ways. When we see ourselves as Christ's, we know that we are his eyes to see needs even if the outer person seems affluent or defiant or unlovable. We feel, like Ed, that our hands are Christ's hands to help and heal and lift. We feel that our feet are Christ's to go on his errand to the needy, the lonely, and the suffering. And most of all, we know that he goes with us.

I feel to end by repeating again the words of benediction I have already quoted that the Apostle Paul spoke to the Ephesians—words that are a great promise to our Heavenly Father about our commitment to righteousness and also a great blessing to all who have taken the name of Christ upon them to become his:

> Blessed be the God and Father of our Lord Jesus Christ, who hath blessed us with all spiritual blessings in heavenly places in Christ:
>
> According as he hath chosen us in him before the foundation of the world, that we should be holy and without blame before him in love (Ephesians 1:3–4).

May we also be holy before him. May we also be blameless in love. May we be among "those that are Christ's."

Notes

1. Marian S. Bergin, "It Takes More than Love," *Ensign*, August 1990, p. 21.

2. Mary Ellen Edmunds, "Blessed, Honored Pioneers," *Ensign*, March 1992, p. 37.

3. Gordon B. Hinckley, "An Ensign to the Nations," *Ensign*, November 1989, p. 54.

4. Hiroshi Shirota, letter to Chieko N. Okazaki, March 21, 1992.

5. *My Errand from the Lord: A Personal Study Guide of the Melchizedek Priesthood Quorums of The Church of Jesus Christ of Latter-day Saints, 1976–77* (Salt Lake City: The Church of Jesus Christ of Latter-day Saints, 1976), pp. 154–55.

Index